Cooking in the New South

A Modern Approach To Traditional Southern Fare.

Anne Byrn Phillips

PHOTOGRAPHY BY FLOYD JILLSON

PEACHTREE PUBLISHERS, LIMITED

Published by
PEACHTREE PUBLISHERS, LTD.
494 Armour Circle, N. E., Atlanta, Georgia 30324

Copyright © 1984 Anne Byrn Phillips

Manufactured in the United States of America

Design by Cynthia McDaniel

First edition

Library of Congress Catalog Number 83-63501

ISBN: 0-931948-52-5

*This cookbook is dedicated
to those people whom I love
the most — my husband, Chris;
my parents, Bebe and Bill Byrn;
and my sisters, Ginger and Susan Byrn.
After all, they survived creamed tuna and peas.*

Contents

Introduction

When I think back on the Southern food I grew up eating in Nashville, Tennessee, it is mostly the fried chicken and milk gravy, turnip greens slowly simmered with ham hocks on New Year's Day, and fresh biscuits and breads — always homemade — that come to mind.

Those were comforting foods to me, foods which Southerners have cooked for generations and hopefully will continue to prepare. But with the aid of today's time-saving appliances, the availability of once hard-to-find ingredients, and our increased travel, Southerners are branching out into a changed style of cookery. We're using the same basic ingredients, but we have altered preparation and presentation, with an emphasis on the light, the simple, and the natural.

It is with *old* Southern cooking and *new* Southern cooking in mind that I write this cookbook, a new look at what is traditional in our kitchens. To preserve the old, most chapters open with a vignette about a treasured technique from our past — such as boiling peanuts or baking chess pies. To spotlight the new, my recipes suggest fresh applications of typically Southern ingredients. I've also tossed in a few favorite formulas, not because they have anything to do with the South, but because on today's Southern dinner tables, you're as likely to find Mexican or Italian dishes as you are hoecakes.

Many of these recipes are my own, but many more belong to family, friends, and talented cooks I have met as food editor of the *Atlanta Journal* and *Atlanta Constitution*.

I hope you enjoy (and use) this cookbook as much as I have enjoyed bringing together the old and the new.

Anne Byrn Phillips
Atlanta, Georgia

Appetizers & Beverages

Boiling Peanuts, Southern-Style

The taste for boiled peanuts is something you have to acquire — not even Southerners are born with it. When I finally acquired the taste seven years ago, it was a true awakening. What I thought would be mushy, salty peanuts, not the least bit similar to their cousins, roasted peanuts, were in fact slightly sweet, crunchy, and had only a faint, salty aftertaste. I found that my visits to north Georgia demanded stopping at roadside boiled peanut stands, and soon I was determined to boil them myself.

In fact, one of the reasons I married my husband, Chris, was that he owned a massive cast-iron washpot, just the size to hold a half-bushel of simmering peanuts.

We boil peanuts together throughout the year. The best time is in the fall, when you can get freshly-dug, Georgia green peanuts. Other times you have to settle for smaller Mexican peanuts.

To boil peanuts in the true Southern style, you bring a half pot of water to a boil and add a half cup of salt per pound of peanuts. When the water is boiling, add the peanuts. Cook them about four hours at a slow simmer, replenishing the fire with wood, when needed. Taste the peanuts occasionally, and cook them longer if you prefer a mushy goober. I prefer peanuts cooked to a firm, but tender consistency, much like pasta.

The most inexpensive way to purchase green peanuts is by the bushel — 42 pounds. When peanuts are the only appetizer at a gathering, allow about one-half pound per person.

You can easily increase the saltiness of boiled peanuts by adding more salt, but you can never decrease it, so be careful.

Quick Pâté

Ingredients for about 3 cups:
1 lb. chicken livers
chicken broth
2 tsp. salt
pinch cayenne pepper
¾ tsp. dry mustard
¼ tsp. allspice
¼ tsp. white pepper
2 Tbl. minced onion
½ cup soft butter
2 Tbl. dry sherry

Directions:
Cover chicken livers with chicken broth and bring to a boil in a medium saucepan. Reduce heat. Simmer 20 minutes, covered, until cooked. Drain well. Place livers in bowl of food processor with remaining ingredients, except sherry. Blend well. Fold in sherry. Pack mixture in crock. Chill.

Note:
   This pâté freezes well. It should come to room temperature before serving with French bread or crackers.

Crusty Havarti

Ingredients for 4 servings:
1 7-oz. round, creamy Havarti cheese *or* Brie cheese
1 Tbl. Dijon-style mustard
3 frozen patty shells *or* ½ sheet frozen puff pastry
water
1 egg, lightly beaten

Directions:
Spread top of cheese with mustard. Set aside. Arrange patty shells close together in triangle. Moisten touching edges with water. Pinch together. Roll dough out to 9-inch circle. Place cheese in center of circle, mustard side down. Gather pastry edges over cheese. Moisten edges and pinch together. Place on greased foil in shallow baking pan, seam side down. Brush all over with beaten egg. Roll scraps into design and arrange on top. Chill 30 minutes. Preheat oven to 375°. Brush again with egg. Arrange foil closely around side of cheese. Bake for 15 minutes. Brush again with egg. Bake 15 minutes more, or until golden brown. Cool 30 minutes on rack. Serve warm as an appetizer with fruit.

Note:
   This recipe comes from the Danish Cheese Association. Substitute sautéed, chopped mushrooms for mustard if desired.

Chris' Jalapeno Oysters

Ingredients for 4 servings:
1 pint oysters, drained, reserve liquor
3 Tbl. butter
3 Tbl. liquid from pickled jalapeno
   peppers
liquor reserved from oysters
jalapeno peppers, sliced, for garnish

Directions:
In colander drain oysters, catching liquor in bowl underneath. Set aside. In small skillet, melt butter. Add jalapeno juice. Mix well. Add oysters to skillet. Poach in mixture until edges just begin to curl, about 1 minute. Add reserved liquor, if needed. (Some oysters are more watery than others.) Scatter pepper slices over oyster mixture. Serve at once with French bread to sop the juices and beer to cool the fire.

Note:
   Chris developed this recipe with a hankering for something hot and spicy, and a pint of oysters and a jar of jalapeno peppers from the refrigerator. It's best with freshly shucked oysters.

Whole Wheat Cheese Straws

Ingredients for 5 dozen:
1 lb. top-quality, sharp Cheddar cheese,
   shredded
1 cup whole wheat flour
1 cup unbleached white flour
1 heaping tsp. cayenne pepper
¾ cup unsalted butter, softened
salt

Directions:
Combine all ingredients except salt in food processor (you will have enough for 2 batches) or by hand. Process until mixture comes together in a ball. Chill about 30 minutes. Preheat oven to 350°. Roll out dough about ¼-inch thick. Cut into strips or rounds. Bake on ungreased baking sheets for about 15 minutes, or until golden brown. Sprinkle with salt while still hot. Serve hot with cocktails or cold with tomato soup.

Note:
   Any Southern cookbook includes at least one recipe for cheese straws. So what sets one cheese straw recipe off from another? For superior cheese straws, you must use a top-quality cheese, preferably from Vermont or New York, although raw-milk Cheddar (such as from Atlanta's R. L. Mathis Dairy) works extremely well and gives the straws a bite. Also, you must season them well with hot pepper. Most men prefer this recipe, because the cheese straws are zingy.

Pickled Shrimp

Ingredients for 8 servings:
1½ lbs. large shrimp, shelled and deveined
water
1 cup Vidalia onions, sliced
1 cup parsley, minced
⅔ cup vegetable oil
⅓ cup cider vinegar
¼ cup sugar
2 cloves garlic, minced
2 tsp. salt
black pepper, to taste

Directions:
Cook shrimp in boiling water until they turn pink, no longer. Drain and set aside. In large bowl, combine shrimp with onions and parsley. Toss to mix. Chill. In small saucepan, combine remaining ingredients. Heat until sugar dissolves. Pour over shrimp mixture. Chill at least 2 hours before serving.

Note:
    This is a great do-ahead dish for tailgate picnics or for the holidays.

Cajun Glazed Mushrooms

Ingredients for 6 servings:
1 lb. fresh, whole, small- to medium-sized button mushrooms
¾ cup butter
2 Tbl. black pepper
½ cup Worcestershire sauce
salt, to taste

Directions:
Wash mushrooms. Drain well. In heavy 4-5-quart saucepan, melt butter over low heat. Raise heat to medium. Add mushrooms. Stir to coat well with butter. Add remaining ingredients. Stir to blend. Cover. Raise heat to high. Cook, stirring often to prevent sticking, for about 10 minutes, or until mushrooms are browned and glazed. Remove with slotted spoon, leaving butter in pan.

Note:
    This recipe is from Terry Thompson, a New Orleans cooking instructor. The mushrooms are spicy and are best served on toothpicks with beer.

Curried Pecans

Ingredients for 2 cups:
2 cups pecan halves
1½ Tbl. unsalted butter
2 tsp. seasoning salt
¾ tsp. curry powder

Directions:
Preheat oven to 275°. Spread pecans in shallow baking pan. Dot with butter. Bake 15-20 minutes, or until dark brown and glossy. Stir to coat during cooking. Mix salt and curry, sprinkle over pecans. Stir. Bake another 5 minutes. Spread on paper towels to cool.

Note:
   A touch of curry makes this Southern favorite just a bit more special. These keep about 10 days in an airtight container.

Shrimp Pâté

Ingredients for 4 servings:
4 Tbl. butter
½ lb. small shrimp, cooked and peeled
1 clove garlic, minced
¼ tsp. mace
¼ tsp. or more salt
dash cayenne pepper
2 Tbl. heavy cream *or* half-and-half
1 Tbl. white wine

Directions:
Place all ingredients in container of blender or food processor. Process until smooth. Season with salt and pepper to taste. (Watch the pepper, as it will grow!) Spoon into ramekin; cover with plastic wrap. Refrigerate 24 hours. Let come to room temperature before serving with crackers and cucumber slices.

Marinated Oysters

Ingredients for 4 servings:

2 doz. oysters, shucked, liquor and shells
   reserved

liquor reserved from oysters

1 large onion, thinly sliced

1 lemon, cut crosswise into paper-thin
   slices

¾ cup white wine vinegar

2 bay leaves

2 tsp. pickling spice

1 tsp. salt

⅛ tsp. black pepper

¼ cup parsley, chopped

¼ cup olive oil

lemon and onion slices, to garnish

Directions:

Place oysters and liquor in 12-inch skillet.
Cook, uncovered, over moderate heat 2-3
minutes, until edges just curl. Immediately
pour contents of pan into fine sieve. Set over
large bowl and let drain. Set aside liquor.
Arrange oysters in one layer in glass dish.
Scatter lemon and onion evenly over top. Set
aside.

In stainless steel or enamel saucepan,
combine vinegar, oyster liquor, bay leaves,
and pickling spice. Bring to boil. Reduce
heat. Simmer 8 minutes. Strain mixture.
Cool to room temperature. Pour over
oysters. Season with remaining ingredients,
except olive oil. Add olive oil. Mix well.

Cover with plastic wrap. Refrigerate 2 days.

Serve oysters piled back into their shells,
with slices of onion and lemon scattered on
top. Serve with toothpicks or cocktail forks.

Note:

I first tasted this recipe at the 1982
National Food Editor's Conference. It is
from the Grotto Restaurant in Seattle,
Washington, and originally was made with
oysters from Northwestern waters. I find it
works very well with the oysters that are so
famous to the South — those from Apala-
chicola Bay.

Sausage Pinwheels

Ingredients for 3 dozen:
2 cups flour
½ tsp. salt
2 tsp. baking powder
2 Tbl. white cornmeal
¼ cup vegetable shortening
¾ cup plus 1 Tbl. milk
1 lb. hot-flavored sausage, room temperature

Directions:
Combine dry ingredients in mixing bowl. Cut in shortening with 2 knives until coarse crumbs form. Add milk. Mix well. Knead dough about 1 minute on floured surface. Divide dough into 2 parts. Roll each into ¼-inch thick square. Spread each with ½ lb. sausage. Roll up from one end. Refrigerate 1 hour. Preheat oven to 375°. Slice ½-inch thick. Place on ungreased cookie sheets. Bake 15-20 minutes, or until golden brown.

Note:
    This is a favorite holiday recipe from my grandmother, Eliza Carr.

Crab Mousse

Ingredients for 10 servings:
¼ cup chicken stock, room temperature
2 ¼-oz. envelopes unflavored gelatin
1½ cups hot chicken stock
1 cup sour cream
1 cup mayonnaise
2 Tbl. minced pimiento
2 Tbl. green onion, minced
3 cups crab, shredded
1½ tsp. white pepper
lemon juice, to taste
salt, to taste
pimiento strips, for garnish

Directions:
Pour room temperature chicken stock in top of double boiler. Sprinkle gelatin over surface. Allow to soften 5 minutes at room temperature. Cook over boiling water until dissolved. Add hot stock. Pour into mixing bowl. Cool. With whisk, blend in sour cream, mayonnaise, pimiento, green onion, crab, and white pepper. Mix. Taste for seasoning. Add lemon juice and salt, if needed.
    Rub inside of 2-quart ring mold with oil. Pour mousse mixture into mold. Chill overnight. Serve garnished with pimiento strips, and accompanied with homemade mayonnaise.

Good Luck Dip

Ingredients for 10 servings:
1¾ cups dried black-eyed peas
5 cups water
5 jalapeno peppers, seeded and chopped
⅓ cup onion, chopped
1 clove garlic
1 cup butter, melted
1 4-oz. can chopped green chiles,
  drained; reserve juice
1 Tbl. chile juice, reserved from can
2 cups Monterey jack cheese, shredded
tomatoes, chopped, to garnish
tortilla chips, to serve

Directions:
Cover peas with water. Boil 2 minutes. Turn off heat. Let soak in liquid 1 hour. Drain. Combine with 5 cups water. Boil, then simmer 1¼ hours, or until tender. Add peppers, onion, and garlic. Preheat oven to 325°. Transfer mixture to blender or food processor. Purée. Add melted butter. Mix well. Pour mixture into baking dish. Top with chiles and liquid. Add cheese. Heat in oven until cheese melts, about 12 minutes. Top with tomatoes. Serve with chips.

Note:
   Use the same procedure to make use of leftover, cooked black-eyed peas. Start with "Add peppers, onion, and garlic. . . ."

Salsa

Ingredients for 3 cups:
2 cups canned, chopped tomatoes,
  undrained
1 medium onion, chopped
1 4-oz. can green chiles, drained and
  diced
1 jalapeno pepper, seeded, deveined and
  chopped
3 cloves garlic, minced
3 Tbl. red wine vinegar
1 Tbl. fresh cilantro, chopped *or* 1 tsp.
  dried cilantro
2 tsp. olive oil
tortilla chips, to serve

Directions:
Mix all ingredients except tortilla chips. Chill, covered. Refrigerate at least a day, then let stand at room temperature 2 hours, before serving. Serve with tortilla chips.

Note:
   This also makes an excellent topping for scrambled eggs, tacos, and hamburgers. Will keep 1 week. It is one of those foreign dishes which has found its way onto Southern tables. In the Lone Star State, salsa is known as "Texas mayonnaise."

Potted Cheddar

Ingredients for 4 cups:
4 cups extra-sharp Cheddar cheese, shredded
4 Tbl. butter
4 Tbl. port
¼ tsp. paprika

Directions:
Blend all ingredients in a blender or food processor until smooth. Put mixture in crock. Cover and refrigerate at least 12 hours, before serving. Serve with sesame seed crackers.

Note:
This improves with age.

Beer Croutons

Ingredients for 12 servings:
1 1-lb. loaf dense, unsliced white bread
1 12-oz. can beer, cold
1 cup Parmesan cheese, grated

Directions:
Preheat oven to 450°. Remove crust from bread. Cut into ½-inch cubes. Dip cubes into cold beer and then cheese. Place on buttered baking sheet. Bake 10-12 minutes, or until golden brown. Serve in a bowl with cocktails or serve atop soup.

Note:
This recipe came from an *Atlanta Weekly* article on cooking with beer. Although most people just drink it, beer is quite useful in cooking; it can be added to marinades to tenderize meat, or added to foods such as these croutons for flavor.

Brie with Pecans

Ingredients for 4 servings:
1 7-oz. round Brie cheese
2 Tbl. unsalted butter
¼ cup pecans, chopped and toasted
1 Tbl. brandy

Directions:
Place Brie 3-4 inches under broiler. Broil 2-3 minutes, or until soft. Melt butter in small skillet. Add pecans and brandy. Pour over hot cheese. Serve with crackers or crusty French bread.

Note:
To toast pecans, spread on baking sheet and heat at 325° for 10 minutes.

Steak on Sticks

Ingredients for 6 servings:
2 lbs. beef flank steak
½ cup soy sauce
4 Tbl. honey
4 Tbl. vegetable oil
2 Tbl. dry red wine
2 cloves garlic, minced
¼ tsp. powdered ginger
salt, to taste
pepper, to taste

Directions:
Partially freeze meat. Thinly slice (less than ½ inch thick) on the diagonal. Combine remaining ingredients in small bowl. Mix well. Place meat in glass dish. Pour marinade over meat. Cover with plastic wrap. Refrigerate and marinate for a day or overnight. Turn occasionally. Thread meat on metal shish kebab skewers. Broil or grill about 3-5 minutes per side, until done. Don't overcook.

Irish Coffee

Ingredients for each drink:
2 Tbl. Irish whiskey
1 heaping tsp. brown sugar
strong coffee, freshly brewed
whipped cream

Directions:
Set wine globets near fire to warm. When ready to drink, place whiskey in goblet. Add brown sugar. Stir well. Add hot coffee to within ¾ inch of top. Stir to mix. Prop stirring spoon against rim of glass and trickle cream down spoon. Layer of cream will float on top.

Note:
  Irish coffees, a sure way to take the chill off a winter night, should be made one at a time.

Margaritas

Ingredients for 4 servings:
4 cups ice cubes
1 cup gold tequila
½ cup triple sec *or* grand Marnier
½ cup fresh lime juice
coarse salt
lime slices, for garnish

Directions:
In pitcher combine ice, tequila, triple sec, and lime juice. Dip rims of 4 glasses into water, then salt. Pour drink into glasses. Garnish with lime slices.

Mulled Cider

Ingredients for 2 quarts:
2 quarts apple cider
4 3-inch cinnamon sticks
1 Tbl. whole cloves
1 tsp. ground ginger
½ tsp. allspice
6 pieces orange peel

Directions:
In stock pot, combine all ingredients. Simmer 30 minutes. Cool and strain. Cover and refrigerate overnight. Reheat and serve in mugs.

Note:
There's no better way to scent a holiday house than with mulled cider on the stove.

Bloody Marys

Ingredients for 6 servings:
46 oz. vegetable-tomato juice
1 Tbl. caraway seeds
1 Tbl. Dijon-style mustard
2 tsp. celery salt
2 Tbl. Worcestershire sauce
juice of 1 lemon
½ tsp. white pepper
2 tsp. black pepper
¼ tsp. garlic powder
3 drops Tabasco sauce
2 tsp. prepared horseradish
¼ tsp. cumin seeds
1 cup vodka
cucumber slices, to garnish

Directions:
In pitcher mix all ingredients, except vodka and cucumber slices. Before serving, fill 6 glasses with ice and vodka. Pour tomato juice mixture over. Garnish with cucumber slices.

Note:
This was adapted from George Baker's recipe from the Bloody Mary Mix-Off in Atlanta.

Christmas Eggnog

Ingredients for 25 1-cup servings:
6 egg yolks
½ cup sugar
½ cup dark rum
1 pint bourbon *or* brandy
2 tsp. vanilla extract
pinch nutmeg
3 cups whipping cream
2 cups milk
6 egg whites
3 Tbl. sugar
nutmeg, to garnish

Directions:
Beat egg yolks until light yellow. Gradually add ½ cup sugar. Continue beating while adding rum and bourbon. Add vanilla extract and nutmeg. Chill 3 hours. Add cream and milk, a little at a time, while mixture chills. Before serving, beat egg whites with 3 Tbl. sugar, until stiff. Fold in eggnog mixture. Sprinkle top with nutmeg and serve.

Note:
This tonic is rich and potent, so you really need only 1 cup per person.

Trader Vic's Champagne Punch

Ingredients for 4 to 5 servings:
cracked ice
1 orange, sliced
½ lemon, sliced
3 slices fresh *or* canned pineapple
1½ oz. maraschino liqueur
1½ oz. chartreuse
1½ oz. brandy
1 bottle champagne

Directions:
Half fill large glass pitcher with cracked ice. Add all ingredients, except champagne. Chill well. Add champagne at last minute. Serve in champagne glasses.

Note:
From a refreshing afternoon at Trader Vic's in Atlanta. We forgot it was 98° outside.

Kim's Piña Colada

Ingredients for 4 servings:
1 cup pineapple juice
6 oz. rum
1 banana, peeled
¾ cup cream of coconut
½ cup crushed pineapple, drained
   (optional)
½ cup shredded coconut (optional)
crushed ice

Directions:
Place all ingredients, except crushed ice, in blender. Fill to top with crushed ice. Blend well, until it has a milkshake texture.

Note:
   From Kim Hoagland, Lanier Sailing Academy.

Glogg

Ingredients for 8 to 10 servings:
3 sticks cinnamon
20 whole cloves
1 cup water
1 cup raisins
⅔ cup slivered almonds
¼ cup sugar
1 half-gallon red wine
1 fifth port
1 cup light rum
1 cup aquavit
orange slices, for garnish

Directions:
In small saucepan, combine cinnamon sticks, cloves, and water. Cover. Bring to a boil. Reduce heat. Simmer about 30 minutes. Strain. Discard spices. In 4-quart pan, combine spiced water with remaining ingredients, except orange slices. Heat over medium-low heat. *Don't* boil. Serve in punch bowl or from copper stock pot. Garnish top of punch with orange slices.

Note:
   This punch tastes good, but it's a killer. From Danish cheese dinner at Food Editor's Conference; now a Christmas open house staple.

Breads

The Art of Making Biscuits

Just as a craftsman takes raw wood and saws, sands, and hammers it into a fine chair, a good cook takes flour, baking powder, shortening, and milk, and creates heavenly biscuits.

In her classic 1928 cookbook, Mrs. S. R. Dull said, "The Southern housewife has always prided herself on the whiteness and flakiness of her biscuits." It's true; we in the South have always been able to produce those flaky, round biscuits — baked high and stuffed with a sausage patty or just butter and homemade preserves — because we bake with soft wheat flour. This flour has less gluten (protein) than harder, northern flours, which are more suitable for baking crusty loaves of bread.

While the traditional biscuits are white, today's variations include whole wheat, hot pepper and cheese, orange, and even rye. The most common recipes call for baking powder and whole milk and rely on a large amount of shortening to make them short, or flaky.

Here are some tips to making better biscuits, no matter which recipe you choose:

Begin with the best ingredients, such as soft flour, chilled shortening (either vegetable, butter, or lard), your choice of liquid, and some leavening.

Cut the shortening into the dry ingredients with a pastry blender or 2 sharp knives. The mixture should look like coarse crumbs. Although a bit tedious, this process assures that your biscuits will rise. It's the moisture in the shortening that turns to steam in the oven and causes the dough to form flaky layers.

Add only enough liquid to make the dough workable, then lightly knead the dough on a floured surface only one minute. Gently roll out the dough and cut rounds with a biscuit cutter or a glass rim, dipped in flour. Press down firmly; if you twist the cutter, the biscuits will turn out lopsided.

Bake the biscuits on ungreased baking sheets. Place them close together for soft-sided biscuits, or an inch apart for crusty-sided biscuits. Bake the biscuits at 450°, unless the recipe says otherwise.

To reheat baked biscuits, place them in aluminum foil and heat at 300° 10-12 minutes.

Mile-High Biscuits

Ingredients for 16 biscuits:
3 cups flour, sifted
2 Tbl. sugar
4½ tsp. baking powder
¾ tsp. cream of tartar
¾ tsp. salt
¾ cup vegetable shortening
1 egg, beaten
¾ cup milk

Directions:
Preheat oven to 450°. In mixing bowl, sift together dry ingredients. Cut in shortening, until mixture resembles coarse meal. In another bowl, combine egg and milk. Beat lightly with fork. Add to flour mixture all at once, stirring enough to make soft dough.

Turn out onto floured board, knead 15 times. Roll out to 1-inch thickness. Cut into 2-inch rounds. Place on ungreased baking sheet about 1 inch apart. Bake 12-15 minutes, or until golden.

Note:
These rise to great proportions. The trick is the beaten egg.

Whole Wheat Biscuits

Ingredients for 2 dozen biscuits:
1 cup flour, sifted
¾ cup whole wheat flour, sifted
½ tsp. salt
3 tsp. baking powder
½ tsp. baking soda
4-5 Tbl. unsalted butter
1 tsp. honey
⅔-¾ cup buttermilk

Directions:
Preheat oven to 450°. In mixing bowl, sift together dry ingredients. Cut in butter, until mixture resembles coarse crumbs. Add honey and enough buttermilk to make soft dough.

Turn dough out on floured board. Knead about 1 minute. Pat out to ½-inch thickness. Cut out into 1½-inch rounds. Place on ungreased baking sheet. Bake 10-12 minutes.

Note:
This is undoubtedly my favorite biscuit.

Angel Biscuits

Ingredients for 3 to 4 dozen:
1 package active dry yeast
2 Tbl. warm water
5 cups flour, sifted *after* measuring
1 tsp. baking soda
1 Tbl. baking powder
4 Tbl. sugar
1 tsp. salt
1 cup vegetable shortening
1½-2 cups buttermilk
melted butter

Directions:
Preheat oven to 400°. Dissolve yeast in water. Sift flour with other dry ingredients. Cut in shortening. Add buttermilk, a little at a time, and yeast mixture to flour mixture. Combine well, adding more buttermilk or flour as necessary to make a soft, yet workable dough. Knead gently for a few minutes on a floured board. Roll out to ½-inch thickness. Cut with biscuit cutters. Brush with melted butter. Place on lightly greased baking sheet (far apart for crisp-sided biscuits and close together for soft-sided biscuits) and bake 12-15 minutes. Dough keeps several days in refrigerator.

Note:
From Holly Wulfing, chef at the Georgia Governor's Mansion.

Cranberry Lemon Bread

Ingredients for 1 loaf (9-by-5-by-3-inch pan):
4 Tbl. butter, softened
¾ cup sugar
2 eggs
2 tsp. lemon rind, grated
2 cups flour, sifted
2½ tsp. baking powder
1 tsp. salt
¾ cup milk
1 cup fresh cranberries, chopped
½ cup pecans, chopped
2 tsp. lemon juice
2 Tbl. sugar

Directions:
Preheat oven to 350°. Cream together butter and ¾ cup sugar in mixing bowl, until light and fluffy. Add eggs one at a time. Add lemon rind. Beat well. Sift together flour, baking powder, and salt. Add to batter alternately with milk. Beat until smooth. Fold in cranberries and pecans. Pour batter into greased 9-by-5-by-3-inch pan. Bake about 55-60 minutes. Cool in pan 10 minutes. Turn out onto rack. When completely cool, combine lemon juice and sugar. Spoon over top. Wrap well.

Note:
Best when served the day after baking, so flavors have a chance to mingle.

Lemon Tea Bread

Ingredients for 1 loaf (9-by-5-by-3-inch
  pan):
6 Tbl. butter, softened
1 cup sugar
2 eggs
½ cup milk
1½ cups flour
1 tsp. baking powder
¼ tsp. salt
½ cup walnuts, chopped
rind of 1 lemon

Ingredients for Glaze:
½ cup sugar
juice of 1 lemon

Directions:
Preheat oven to 350°. In mixing bowl, cream
butter and 1 cup sugar. Add eggs. Beat well.
Add milk, flour, baking powder, and salt.
Stir in nuts and lemon rind. Pour batter into
greased loaf pan. Bake 50-55 minutes, or
until bread tests done.
    Combine glaze ingredients. Spoon over
bread immediately after removing from
oven.

Note:
    From Kathy Wages of the Clayton
County (Georgia) Extension Service.

Date Nut Bread

Ingredients for 1 loaf (9-by-5-by-3-inch
  pan):
2 cups dates, chopped
2 Tbl. vegetable shortening
⅔ cup brown sugar
½ cup honey
¾ tsp. vanilla extract
¾ cup hot water
¼ cup orange juice
1 egg, beaten
2 cups flour, sifted
1 tsp. baking soda
1 tsp. salt
1 cup walnuts, chopped

Directions:
Preheat oven to 325°. Place dates, shortening, sugar, honey, vanilla extract, hot water,
and juice in a mixing bowl. Stir to combine.
Set aside 15 minutes. Add egg to date
mixture. Mix well. Stir in flour, baking soda,
and salt. Stir only enough to moisten dry
ingredients. Fold in nuts.
    Turn batter into greased loaf pan. Bake 1
hour. Test for doneness with toothpick. Let
stand in pan 10 minutes after baking. Turn
onto rack to cool. Cool before slicing. Can
use greased, 1-lb. coffee cans instead of loaf
pans. Serve with cream cheese.

Note:
    From Merijoy Rucker of Alpharetta,
who caters, teaches cooking classes, and is
especially talented at baking breads.

Pumpkin Raisin Bread

Ingredients for 2 regular loaves *or* 6 to 8
  mini-loaves:
3 cups sugar
1 cup vegetable oil
4 eggs, beaten
1 16-oz. can pumpkin
3½ cups flour, sifted
2 tsp. baking soda
2 tsp. salt
1 tsp. baking powder
1 tsp. nutmeg
1 tsp. allspice
1 tsp. cinnamon
½ tsp. ground cloves
⅔ cup water
1 cup raisins

Directions:
Preheat oven to 350°. Cream sugar and oil.
Add eggs and pumpkin. Mix well. Combine
dry ingredients. Add to pumpkin mixture
alternately with water. Mix well after each
addition. Gently stir in raisins. Pour batter
into 2 regular-sized loaf pans or into 6 to 8
miniature loaf pans, which have been
greased and floured. Bake about 30-40
minutes for the small pans and 50-60 minutes
for larger loaves, or until bread starts to pull
away from sides of pan. Let stand 10
minutes. Remove from pans to cool.

Note:
  Baked in miniature pans, these make
attractive and tasty gifts. Fill a basket with
various mini-loaves of fruit breads for a
Christmas gift. This is excellent cold, and
even better when left to age in the refrigerator for a few days. For a variation, pour the
batter into greased and floured muffin tins
and bake at 400° for 15 minutes. All versions
of this recipe freeze well.

Alma Blueberry Bread

Ingredients for 1 loaf:
2 Tbl. butter
¼ cup boiling water
½ cup orange juice
3 tsp. orange rind, grated
1 egg
1 cup sugar
2 cups flour, sifted
1 tsp. baking powder
¼ tsp. baking soda
½ tsp. salt
1 cup fresh blueberries
2 Tbl. orange juice
1 tsp. orange rind, grated
2 Tbl. honey

Directions:
Preheat oven to 325°. Melt butter in boiling water in small saucepan. Add ½ cup orange juice and 3 tsp. orange rind. Set aside. In mixing bowl, beat egg with sugar, until light and fluffy. In separate bowl, combine flour, baking powder, baking soda, and salt. Add dry ingredients to egg-sugar mixture alternately with orange mixture. Fold in blueberries. Pour batter into large, greased loaf pan. Bake about 1 hour and 10 minutes. Turn bread out onto rack to cool. Mix 2 Tbl. orange juice, 1 tsp. rind, and 2 Tbl. honey together. Pour over bread, while hot. Let stand until cool.

Note:
The sweetest blueberries in the summer come from south Georgia, and Alma is our blueberry capital.

Zucchini Bread

Ingredients for 2 regular-sized loaves *or* 6
  mini-loaves:
2 cups unpeeled, medium-sized zucchini
  squash (about 2-3), grated
¾ cup walnuts, chopped
2 Tbl. flour
3 cups flour
2 tsp. cinnamon
½ tsp. nutmeg
1 tsp. baking soda
1 tsp. baking powder
½ tsp. salt
4 eggs
2 cups sugar
1 cup vegetable oil
1 cup raisins
¾ cup walnuts, chopped

Directions:
Preheat oven to 350°. Combine zucchini with
walnuts and 2 Tbl. flour. Set aside. Sift 3
cups flour with cinnamon and nutmeg, soda,
baking powder, and salt. Set aside. Beat
eggs. Gradually beat in sugar, then oil. With
wooden spoon, blend in a little of the flour
mixture, then some zucchini mixture. Keep
adding these ingredients, until both are
blended into egg mixture. When well mixed,
add raisins and nuts. Don't overmix. Turn
batter into 2 greased and floured loaf pans.
Bake about 55 minutes, or until bread tests
done. Cool 10 minutes in pan. Wrap well, to
store. This freezes well.

Note:
  This zucchini bread can be baked during
the summer months, when zucchini from
your garden is in peak supply, and then
frozen for holiday giving. Try baking it in
mini-loaf pans.

Georgia Shrimp Puppies

Ingredients for 2 dozen small puppies:
1 lb. small shrimp, peeled, cooked and
   chopped
4 water chestnuts, chopped
¼ cup bamboo shoots, chopped
⅛ tsp. garlic powder
⅛ tsp. black pepper
1 egg
2 green onions, chopped
6 Tbl. self-rising flour
2 Tbl. water
¼ tsp. dark sesame oil
1 Tbl. soy sauce
hot oil for frying

Directions:
In mixing bowl, combine all ingredients.
Transfer mixture to blender or food processor. Mix to blend well. Drop mixture by
spoonfuls into hot oil (350°). Fry until
puppies puff up and are brown on all sides,
about 3 minutes.

Note:
   These flavorful puppies are a cross
between an egg roll and a hush puppy. They
work well as bread or as appetizers to dunk
in hot mustard.

Cheddar Raisin Muffins

Ingredients for 1 dozen:
2 cups flour
3½ tsp. baking powder
¾ tsp. salt
6 Tbl. butter
1 cup sharp Cheddar cheese, shredded
1 egg, beaten
1 cup milk
¾ cup raisins

Directions:
Preheat oven to 400°. Sift flour with baking
powder and salt. Cut in butter, until it forms
coarse crumbs. Stir in cheese. Blend egg and
milk. Add to dry mixture, stirring only until
moist. Fold in raisins. Spoon batter into
greased muffin tins, filling ⅔ full. Bake 25
minutes, or until brown. Serve hot.

Note:
   This recipe came from the 1982 National
Food Editor's Conference. You'll find no
better accompaniment to ham, pork chops,
or grilled chicken than these muffins. The
raisins make them sweet; the cheese keeps
them savory.

Peach Muffins

Ingredients for 2 dozen:
1½ cups sugar
½ cup vegetable shortening
2 eggs
2¼ cups puréed, fresh peaches (about 8 medium)
2 cups flour
1 tsp. cinnamon
1 tsp. baking soda
1 tsp. baking powder
¼ tsp. salt
1 tsp. vanilla extract
1 cup pecans, chopped

Directions:
Preheat oven to 375°. In mixing bowl, cream sugar and shortening. Add eggs. Mix well. Add peach purée and dry ingredients. Mix well. Add vanilla extract and nuts. Fold in until all ingredients are moistened. Pour into greased muffin tins; fill ⅔ full. Bake about 20 minutes, or until muffins test done. Let cool before removing from pan.

Note:
    This batter can be baked in a loaf pan at 325° for 50-60 minutes.

Sweet Potato Muffins

Ingredients for 2 dozen muffins:
1¼ cups sugar
1¼ cups fresh *or* canned sweet potatoes, cooked and mashed
½ cup butter, softened
2 eggs, room temperature
1½ cups flour
2 tsp. baking powder
1 tsp. cinnamon
¼ tsp. nutmeg
¼ tsp. salt
1 cup milk
½ cup raisins, chopped
¼ cup walnuts, chopped

Directions:
Preheat oven to 400°. Beat sugar, sweet potatoes, and butter in mixing bowl. Add eggs. Blend well. Sift together flour, baking powder, spices, and salt. Add to mixture alternately with milk, beginning and ending with dry ingredients. Don't overmix. Fold in raisins and nuts. Spoon into greased muffin tins, about ½ full. Bake 25-30 minutes, or until muffins test done.

Note:
    These freeze beautifully.

McTyre's Cornbread

Ingredients for 8 servings:
1½ cups self-rising cornmeal
3 eggs, beaten
1 cup cream-style corn
½ cup vegetable oil
1 cup buttermilk
1 large jalapeno pepper, seeded, deveined, and chopped
½ large green bell pepper, seeded and chopped
1 tsp. salt
1 cup Monterey jack *or* Cheddar cheese, shredded

Directions:
Preheat oven to 375°. Mix all ingredients, except cheese, in mixing bowl. Stir just until ingredients are moistened. Pour half batter into 8- or 9-inch square, greased and floured baking pan. Sprinkle cheese on top. Pour over remaining batter. Bake 45 minutes, or until golden brown.

Note:
From photographer Joe McTyre.

Parmesan Bread

Ingredients for 4 servings:
1 package dry yeast
¼ cup warm water
¼ cup milk, scalded
1½ cups flour, sifted
1 Tbl. sugar
½ tsp. salt
⅓ cup butter
1 egg, beaten
½ cup Parmesan cheese, grated
2 Tbl. parsley, chopped
1 Tbl. green onion, minced
1 Tbl. butter (optional)

Directions:
Dissolve yeast in warm water. Cool scalded milk. Add to yeast mixture. Sift flour with sugar and salt. Cut in butter with 2 knives, until mixture resembles coarse crumbs. Add beaten egg and yeast mixture to flour. Stir well to combine. Add Parmesan cheese, parsley, and onions to batter. Stir well. Pour dough into greased, 9-inch pie plate. Cover with damp cloth. Let rise in warm place until doubled in bulk, about 40 minutes. Preheat oven to 375°. Dot with butter, if desired, and bake 20-25 minutes. Cut into wedges, when slightly cool.

Note:
From Atlanta chef Anita Kidd.

꧁ Pumpkin Cheesecake (page 158), Pumpkin Raisin Bread (page 19)

❧ Irish Coffee (page 11)

Corn Light Bread

Ingredients for 2 regular-sized loaves *or* 6
  mini-loaves:
4 cups stone-ground white cornmeal
1 cup flour
¾ cup sugar
1 tsp. salt
1 tsp. baking soda
4 cups buttermilk
4 Tbl. butter, melted
butter, melted

Directions:
Preheat oven to 350°. Combine dry ingredients in large mixing bowl. Make a well in
center, and gradually mix in buttermilk and 4
Tbl. melted butter, stirring only enough for
ingredients to moisten. Turn batter into
greased loaf pans. Bake 50-60 minutes; or
only 35 minutes for the smaller pans. Brush
with melted butter after baking. Let cool in
pans 5 minutes. Then turn out on racks.

Note:
    This is a Tennessee specialty and often is
served with pork barbecue. It tastes best
while warm, but can be reheated the next
day.

Crisp Cornbread

Ingredients for 6 servings:
1 cup flour
1 Tbl. baking powder
¼ tsp. baking soda
1 tsp. salt
1 cup stone-ground white cornmeal
1 egg
1½ cups buttermilk
4 Tbl. butter, melted

Directions:
Preheat oven to 425°. In medium-sized
mixing bowl, stir together flour, baking
powder, baking soda, and salt. Stir in
cornmeal. In small bowl, beat egg until
foamy. Add buttermilk. Mix well. Stir
egg-buttermilk mixture into dry ingredients.
Beat with spoon until smooth. Stir in butter.
Turn batter into buttered, 9-by-9-by-1¾-
inch, square pan. Bake about 25 minutes, or
until sides shrink away from pan and top is
light brown. Serve with softened butter. This
bread is only about an inch high.

Note:
    For those who don't like dense, thick
cornbread, this is a treat.

Zucchini Spoonbread

Ingredients for 4 servings as an entree *or*
  6 to 8 servings as a side dish:
1½ cups zucchini squash, grated (about 2
  medium zucchini squash)
1 Tbl. unsalted butter
3 cups milk
1 cup white *or* yellow cornmeal
4 Tbl. butter
1 tsp. salt
¼ tsp. black pepper, freshly ground
1½ tsp. fresh oregano, minced *or* ½ tsp.
  dried oregano
½ cup Parmesan cheese, freshly grated
3 eggs, separated, room-temperature
pinch salt

Directions:
Preheat oven to 350°. Place zucchini in
colander. Drain well for at least an hour. In
oven, melt 1 Tbl. butter in 2-quart casserole
for 2-3 minutes. Brush sides and bottom of
casserole with melted butter. Set aside.

   In 5-quart, heavy-bottomed saucepan,
bring milk to boil over medium heat. Add
zucchini. With a wooden spoon and whisk,
gradually stir in cornmeal until dissolved.
Cook over reduced heat, stirring until thick,
2 minutes. Add 4 Tbl. butter, salt, pepper,
oregano, and Parmesan cheese. Mix well.
Cook 2 minutes more. Remove pan from
heat. Add lightly beaten egg yolks.

   In mixing bowl, beat egg whites with salt
until stiff but not dry. Fold into yolk-meal
mixture. Pour batter into buttered casserole
dish. Spread batter evenly, smoothing top
with spatula. Bake, uncovered, 35-40 minutes, until puffed and browned.

Note:
   From my article on spoonbreads in
May/June 1983, *The Cook's Magazine.*

Spoonbread with Corn

Ingredients for 4 servings as an entree *or*
  6 servings as a side dish:
1 Tbl. unsalted butter
1½ cups fresh white corn (about 3 ears),
  cut from the cob
3 cups milk
2 tsp. salt
1 cup white *or* yellow cornmeal
6 Tbl. unsalted butter
1 Tbl. sugar
¼ tsp. nutmeg
¼ tsp. cayenne pepper
3 eggs, separated, room temperature
pinch salt

Directions:
Preheat oven to 350°. Butter bottom and
sides of 2-quart casserole with 1 Tbl. butter.
Place corn, milk, and salt in heavy-bottomed, 5-quart saucepan. Bring to boil over
high heat. Slowly add cornmeal, so that the
boiling continues at rapid rate. Stir with
wooden spoon to keep mixture smooth.
Reduce heat to low. Stir from time to time.
Simmer, uncovered, until mixture is so thick
spoon will just about stand up in middle of
pan, about 5 minutes.

Remove pan from heat. Immediately
add 6 Tbl. butter, sugar, nutmeg, and
cayenne pepper. Incorporate lightly beaten
egg yolks into mixture. Beat egg whites with
salt until stiff but not dry. Fold into cornmeal
mixture. Pour batter into casserole. Spread
evenly, smoothing over top with a spatula.
Bake, uncovered, 40-45 minutes, or until
puffed and golden.

Note:
This recipe originally came from Anita
Kidd of Atlanta; I reworked it a little and
used it as part of an article on spoonbreads in
May/June 1983, *The Cook's Magazine*.

Stone Mtn. Whole Wheat Bread

Ingredients for 2 loaves (9-by-5-by-3-inch pan):
2½ cups warm water
3 Tbl. honey
2 tsp. salt
¼ cup vegetable oil
1 package active dry yeast, dissolved in ¼ cup lukewarm water
3 cups whole wheat flour
4½ cups unbleached flour

Directions:
Mix warm water with honey, salt, and oil. Add dissolved yeast. Set aside. Stir flours together in large mixing bowl. Make well in center. Pour in yeast mixture. Work batter together with hands or wooden spoon. Knead until smooth and elastic. Place dough in greased bowl, turn over to grease top. Cover. Let rise in warm place until doubled in bulk, about 2 hours. Knead briefly. Divide into 2 balls. Form balls into loaves. Place in greased loaf pans. Cover. Let rise until almost doubled in bulk. This takes about 1½ hours. Preheat oven to 375°. Bake 40-45 minutes. Cover with foil the last 15 minutes, if needed. For a pretty finish, brush loaf with milk before baking.

Note:
From Basket Bakery, Stone Mountain, Georgia.

Bebe's Basic Bread Dough

Ingredients for 3 to 4 dozen:
2 cups flour
¾ cup sugar
1½ tsp. salt
2 packages dry yeast
1 cup milk
⅔ cup water
¼ cup butter
2 eggs
¾ cup flour
2¼-3¼ cups flour

Directions:
In large mixing bowl, combine 2 cups of the flour, sugar, salt, and undissolved yeast. Combine milk, water, and butter in small saucepan. Heat until warm (about 115°). Gradually add to dry ingredients. With electric mixer, beat 2 minutes at medium speed. Add eggs and ¾ cup more flour. Beat on high 2 minutes. Stir in enough additional flour to make stiff dough (about 2¼-3¼ cups). Turn out onto floured board. Knead 10 minutes. Cover with plastic wrap, then tea towel. Let rest 20 minutes. Place in refrigerator 24 hours. Next day, preheat oven to 375°. Roll out dough 1-inch thick. Cut into shapes for rolls. Bake rolls 25 minutes.

Note:
This basic recipe can be braided in a wreath to encompass a wheel of Brie. You can also roll dough into rectangle, brush with melted butter, and sprinkle with brown sugar and cinnamon. Roll into "jellyroll." Cut crosswise into slices, place in pan and bake 20 minutes.

Honey Whole Wheat Rolls

Ingredients for 2 dozen rolls *or* 1 loaf:
1 package active dry yeast
¼ cup very warm water (115°)
1 tsp. honey
2 cups milk
1 Tbl. vegetable oil
2 Tbl. honey
2 tsp. salt
2 cups whole wheat flour
3 cups flour, sifted
1 egg white
water
3 Tbl. sesame seeds

Directions:
Sprinkle yeast over very warm water in cup measure. Stir in 1 tsp. honey. Stir until yeast is dissolved. Let mixture stand 10 minutes, until bubbly. Heat milk in saucepan to lukewarm. Pour into large mixing bowl. Stir in oil, 2 Tbl. honey, salt, and yeast mixture. Blend. Add whole wheat flour. Beat vigorously for 2 minutes or until smooth. Add enough white flour to make soft dough or until dough comes away from side of bowl. Turn dough out onto floured board. Knead 10 minutes or until dough is soft and elastic.

Press dough into greased bowl. Cover with damp cloth. Let rise in warm place until doubled in bulk, about 1 hour. Then, punch dough down. Knead slightly on lightly floured board. Let rest 5 minutes. Shape into rolls or loaf of bread. Place on ungreased baking sheets. Brush rolls with egg white (beaten with water until foamy). Sprinkle with sesame seeds. Let rise until doubled in bulk. Bake at 375° 20-30 minutes, or until golden brown.

Note:
A good, basic whole wheat bread recipe from Merijoy Rucker of Alpharetta.

Herren's Sweet Rolls

Ingredients for 5 to 6 dozen rolls:
1 cup milk
¼ cup butter
¼ cup sugar
1¼ tsp. salt
2 packages active dry yeast
¼ cup warm water
4 cups flour, sifted
butter, melted
2 cups sugar
4 Tbl. cinnamon

Directions:
Let milk come to boil in heavy saucepan. Add butter, sugar, and salt. Cool. Soften yeast in warm water. Stir into milk mixture. Add flour, a little at a time, to liquid mixture. Beat well. Turn out onto floured board. Allow to sit 15 minutes. Knead until smooth and satiny.

Place dough in greased bowl. Turn over once. Cover with cloth. Let rise in warm place until doubled in size. Roll out dough on floured board to about ¼-inch thickness. Cut into rough, 8-inch squares. Work with 1 square at a time. Brush with melted butter.

Mix sugar with cinnamon. Sprinkle most of this mixture generously over entire surface. Starting at one side of square, roll into tube. Continue rolling back and forth, until 12-18 inches long. Cut into wheels about ½-inch wide. Place wheels on baking sheet that has been brushed with melted butter and sprinkled well with cinnamon-sugar mixture. Place them so that they touch. Brush tops with melted butter and more cinnamon-sugar mixture. Let stand, covered, at room temperature for 1 hour to rise again.

Bake at 350° 18-20 minutes. You can refrigerate rolls, covered, and then bring back to room temperature for 30 minutes before baking.

Note:
Herren's restaurant serves the best-known rolls in Atlanta.

The Best Turkey Dressing

Ingredients for 12 to 14 servings:
6 Tbl. butter
2½ cups onions, finely chopped
6 Tbl. butter
3 tart apples, chopped
1 lb. pork sausage
3 cups cornbread, coarsely crumbled
3 cups whole wheat bread, coarsely
  crumbled
3 cups sourdough *or* French bread,
  coarsely crumbled
1½ tsp. dried thyme
1 scant tsp. dried sage
salt, to taste
black pepper, freshly ground, to taste
½ cup parsley, chopped
1 cup pecans, chopped
2 eggs, lightly beaten
chicken *or* turkey stock, to moisten

Directions:
Melt 6 Tbl. butter in large frying pan. Add onions. Cook over medium heat, until onions are quite soft and tender, about 15 minutes. Transfer onions and butter to large mixing bowl. Set aside. Melt another 6 Tbl. butter in same frying pan. Add apple. Cook over medium heat, until lightly colored but not mushy. Transfer apples and butter to mixing bowl with onions.

Crumble sausage into frying pan. Cook over medium heat, until lightly browned. With a slotted spoon, transfer sausage to mixing bowl. Reserve fat. Add remaining ingredients, except eggs and stock, to mixing bowl. Mix well. Add eggs. Mix. Add enough stock to bowl to make moist but not runny mixture. Add fat to stuffing if desired. Let cool slightly. Stuff 20-lb. turkey. If cooking dressing separately from turkey, pour fat over dressing in casserole. Bake at 325° for 30-45 minutes.

Note:
This dressing, adapted from "The Silver Palate Cookbook," is always a hit. It is rich, so no other bread is needed on the Thanksgiving table. Cook your turkey about 12-15 minutes per lb. at 325°, basting frequently.

Bread Sticks

Ingredients for 4 servings:
4 large sourdough rolls, cut into halves
   lengthwise
4 cloves garlic, mashed
olive oil *or* butter, softened
2 cups Parmesan cheese, grated

Directions:
Preheat oven to 400°. Rub roll halves with garlic. Either pour a little olive oil into saucer and dip halves into oil, *or* spread halves lightly with softened butter. Cut each half into 3-4 sticks. Sprinkle cheese over sticks. Place on foil-lined cookie sheet. Bake about 5 minutes, or until cheese melts.

Parmesan Cheese Loaf

Ingredients for 4 servings:
1 loaf of crusty French bread, at least 14
   inches long
2 Tbl. olive oil
2 Tbl. parsley, finely chopped
1 tsp. garlic, finely chopped
2 Tbl. Parmesan cheese, freshly grated

Directions:
Preheat oven to 400°. Split loaf in half lengthwise. Brush each half with 1 Tbl. oil. Sprinkle each half with equal amounts of parsley and garlic. Sprinkle with cheese. At this point, you can wrap the loaf in foil to preheat later (if you do, unwrap the loaf before baking). Place loaf on baking sheet. Bake 10 minutes.

Note:
   Although it doesn't seem like a lot of garlic is going on this bread, it's quite pungent when baked.

Soups & Salads

In a (Brunswick) Stew

When it comes to cooking, we're all authorities. And when it comes to Brunswick stew, every good Southern cook has a different opinion.

As far as I'm concerned, Brunswick stew is one of those culinary mysteries that never should be unfolded. Did it originate in Brunswick County, Virginia, in Brunswick County, North Carolina, or in Brunswick, Georgia? But what does its place of origin matter when the medley of meat, vegetables, and seasonings is one of the best examples of Southern soup creativity?

Brunswick stews are made of rabbits and squirrels, of chickens and pork, and even of beef. They are related to the Kentucky "burgoos," which often use lamb and sometimes okra. Brunswick stews are served at hog roasts because it is the hog's head which flavors the stew so well. The head and feet are placed in boiling water until the meat falls from the bones; the liquor is skimmed and becomes the stock to which meats and vegetables are added.

To assemble a Brunswick stew, you must let your palate be your guide. Decide first on what meat or poultry is at hand, then pick vegetables that complement the meat. For example, corn is particularly tasty with pork, okra with chicken, and potatoes with beef. Tomatoes are absolutely essential. So is plenty of vinegar, either in the form of barbecue sauce or just added at the last to season. Black pepper, too, is a must. Those with weak stomachs never have tolerated Brunswick stew.

When cooking your stew, make sure to keep enough liquor to cover meat and vegetables; if needed, add more liquid to pot. Brunswick stew should be cooked slowly for hours. It should be eaten with a fork, if it has been prepared properly.

Cantaloupe Soup

Ingredients for 4 servings:
1 large ripened cantaloupe, peeled,
   seeded, and cut into pieces
½-¾ cup dry sherry
¼-½ cup sugar
2 Tbl. lime juice
lime, thinly sliced for garnish

Directions:
Place cantaloupe, sherry, sugar, and lime juice in bowl of food processor or blender container. Purée until smooth. Taste for seasoning. Add more sugar, sherry, or lime juice if called for by the size and sweetness of your cantaloupe. Chill thoroughly. Serve garnished with lime slices.

Note:
   A lovely summer soup, as pretty to look at as it is good to eat.

Cucumber-Tomato Soup

Ingredients for 6 servings:
1 large onion, chopped
½ cup butter
4 cups cucumbers, peeled, seeded, and
   chopped
4 cups tomatoes, peeled, seeded, and
   chopped
4 Tbl. flour
4 cups chicken broth
½ cup heavy cream
salt, to taste
pepper, to taste

Directions:
Sauté onion in butter in large skillet. When onions are soft, blend them in batches, along with cucumbers, tomatoes, flour, and broth in blender or food processor, until smooth. Return mixture to skillet. Heat only until warm, stirring. Let cool slightly. Add cream, salt, and pepper. Stir well. Chill.

Note:
   Soup is made even prettier when sprinkled with chopped fresh oregano or basil from your garden.

Simple Gazpacho

Ingredients for 6 servings:
1 quart beef-tomato juice, chilled
¼ cup green onion, minced
¼ cup cucumber, peeled and grated
⅛ tsp. black pepper
⅛ tsp. garlic salt
cherry tomatoes *or* cucumber slices, for
   garnish

Directions:
Place all ingredients, except garnish, in pitcher. Stir well to combine. Pour into 6 glasses. Garnish each with cherry tomato on toothpick or cucumber slices.

Note:
   This is so easy to prepare; keep this mixture in the refrigerator during sultry summer months.

Gazpacho

Ingredients for 4 to 6 servings:
6 large ripe tomatoes, chopped
2 green bell peppers, seeded and chopped
2 medium yellow onions, chopped
1 green onion, chopped
1 clove garlic, minced
2 large cucumbers, peeled, seeded, and
   chopped
½ cup red wine vinegar
½ cup olive oil
1½ cups canned tomato juice
3 eggs, lightly beaten
cayenne pepper, to taste
salt, to taste
black pepper, freshly ground, to taste
⅓ cup fresh dill, chopped

Directions:
In container of blender or bowl of food processor, combine tomatoes, peppers, onions, green onion, garlic, and cucumbers. In small bowl, whisk together vinegar, olive oil, tomato juice, and eggs. Pour mixture into blender or processor. Purée mixture. Season with cayenne pepper, salt, and black pepper. Stir in dill. Chill several hours before serving.

Note:
   Spicy. Serve to dinner guests instead of cocktails.

Chris' Chili

Ingredients for 12 servings:
2 lbs. chuck, coarsely ground
5 medium onions, chopped
5 green onions, chopped
2 red bell peppers, seeded and chopped
3 Tbl. olive oil
8 cloves garlic, minced
2 12-oz. cans beer
black pepper, freshly ground
4 Tbl. fresh chili powder
¼ tsp. ground red pepper
3-4 small, dried hot peppers, crumbled
1 28-oz. can tomatoes
5 fresh tomatoes, chopped
8 oz. vegetable-tomato juice *or* tomato sauce
kidney beans (optional)

Directions:
In heavy soup pot, brown chuck. Stir often. Simultaneously, in medium skillet, sauté onions, green onions, peppers, and garlic in olive oil until soft, about 8 minutes. After beef is browned, add beer to meat, along with black pepper, chili powder, red pepper, crumbled hot peppers, tomatoes and tomato juice. Add sautéed onions, peppers, and garlic to this. Bring mixture to boil. Reduce heat. Cover. Allow to simmer at least 2 hours, adding more liquid if needed. Add kidney beans, as desired. Chris prefers to serve them as a side dish with the chili. Simmer chili another hour. Taste for seasoning. Refrigerate in 2 or 3 portions. Reheat and serve next day.

Note:
Chris insists the key to decent chili is hot peppers, fresh ingredients, the night marination in the refrigerator, and frequent swilling of beer by the cook. I agree.

Basic Chicken Stock

Ingredients for about 6 quarts:
5 lbs. chicken wings
3 lbs. chicken necks *or* backs *or* a
    combination of these parts
1 3-3½-lb. chicken
water
4 sprigs fresh parsley
3 carrots, chopped
2 leeks, quartered
2 celery ribs
2 bay leaves
1 unpeeled onion, chopped
1 tsp. salt
1 tsp. black peppercorns, crushed
½ tsp. dried thyme (optional)

Directions:
Combine wings, chicken parts, and whole chicken in large stock pot with enough water to cover, about 6 quarts. Bring to simmer. Skim off foam as it rises to surface. Reduce heat. Simmer, uncovered, 30 minutes. Add remaining ingredients and partially cover pot. Simmer another 30 minutes, or until whole chicken is cooked. Remove chicken from pot. Set aside to make into chicken salad or casserole. Continue simmering stock another 2½ hours. Strain stock into bowl. Let cool 1 hour at room temperature. Turn stock into 3 or 4 smaller vessels. Cool overnight, uncovered, in refrigerator. When completely chilled, remove layer of fat from surface. Stock is ready to use or to freeze for future use.

Note:
    Freeze stock in small portions — leftover plastic jugs from whipping cream work well. You always must cool stock in small portions. This helps prevent the growth of harmful bacteria.

Ham Hock and Corn Soup

Ingredients for 6 to 8 servings:
2½ quarts chicken stock
1½ lbs. ham hocks, scrubbed and rinsed
¼ cup onion, chopped
½ tsp. black pepper
3 ribs celery, chopped
2 ears corn, each cut into thirds
2 cups cabbage, chopped

Directions:
Combine chicken stock, ham hocks, onion, and pepper in large stock pot. Cover. Simmer 1½-2 hours or until hocks are tender. Remove meat from bones. Cut into small pieces. Discard skin and bones. Return meat to pot with celery. Cook about 15 minutes. Drop corn and cabbage into pot. Cook only 5 minutes more. If soup gets too salty, thin with more stock or water. Adjust seasoning.

Note:
   Serve with hot hoecakes or homemade biscuits, for a truly Southern taste.

Basic Brunswick Stew

Ingredients for 6 servings:
1 3-lb. whole chicken
3 cups water
1½ tsp. salt
1 cup potatoes, diced (optional)
1¾ cups frozen *or* fresh lima beans
1¾ cups tomato sauce
⅔ cup onion, chopped
1¾ cups fresh *or* frozen corn
1 tsp. sugar
salt, to taste
black pepper, freshly ground, to taste
½ tsp. dried basil
½ tsp. dried oregano
¼ tsp. cayenne pepper

Directions:
Simmer chicken in large pot with water and salt until tender, about 2 hours. Drain off broth. Set aside. Remove skin and bones from chicken. Discard. Cut chicken meat into tiny pieces. Skim fat from broth. Return broth to pot. Bring to boil. Reduce broth to 2 cups.
   Add potatoes to broth. Simmer 10 minutes. Add lima beans, tomato sauce, and onion. Cook 20 minutes. Add chicken and remaining ingredients. Cook 15-20 minutes more, or until vegetables are tender.

Note:
   Seasonings can be adjusted according to your taste. Potatoes can be omitted.

Chilled Avocado Soup

Ingredients for 4 servings:
1 medium avocado, pitted, peeled, and
    cut into 1-inch pieces
2 cups milk
2 Tbl. dry sherry
½ tsp. salt
¼-½ tsp. ground cumin
black pepper, to taste
cayenne pepper, to taste
½ cup canned green chiles, minced
¼ cup green onion, minced
tortilla chips, for garnish

Directions:
Place avocado in blender container or food
processor bowl. Purée. Transfer to serving
bowl. Mix in remaining ingredients, except
garnish. Cover bowl. Chill several hours.
Serve with tortilla chips.

Note:
    The more cumin you add to this soup, the
spicier and more Mexican in flavor it
becomes.

Cold Watercress Soup

Ingredients for 4 servings:
2 cups chicken broth
2 cups watercress, washed, dried, and
    chopped (1 bunch)
¼ cup celery, chopped
2 Tbl. Parmesan cheese, grated
dash salt
dash black pepper, freshly ground
2 Tbl. flour
1 cup half-and-half
watercress leaves, for garnish

Directions:
In saucepan, combine chicken broth, watercress, celery, Parmesan cheese, salt, and
pepper. (Be careful not to oversalt if you are
using canned chicken broth). Simmer, uncovered, 10 minutes over moderate heat.
Cool. Pour into a blender jar or bowl of food
processor. Purée at high speed until well
combined and smooth.

    In same saucepan, combine half-and-
half and flour. Warm over moderate heat,
stirring, until slightly thick. Slowly add
puréed watercress mixture, stirring over
heat until thickened. Cool. Chill well. Serve
garnished with fresh watercress.

Seafood Soup

Ingredients for 4 servings:
4 Tbl. unsalted butter
4 large shrimp, peeled
12 sea scallops
1 cup dry white wine
1 cup fish stock *or* bottled clam juice *or* chicken stock
4 Tbl. unsalted butter
2 Tbl. onions, chopped
6 fresh mushrooms, thinly sliced
2 cups heavy cream
2 tsp. lemon juice
4 Tbl. unsalted butter
salt, to taste
black pepper, to taste
12 mussels, scrubbed and steamed
2 tsp. fresh parsley, chopped

Directions:
In large skillet, melt 4 Tbl. butter. Add shrimp and scallops. Cook, stirring, until slightly opaque. Add wine and stock. Bring to boil. Lower heat. Simmer 3 minutes. Remove from heat. Strain seafood from pan and set aside.

In another saucepan, melt 4 Tbl. butter. Add onions and mushrooms. Sauté until onions are translucent. Add reserved stock-wine mixture to pan. Mix well. Stir in cream and lemon juice. Bring mixture to boil over medium heat. Whip 4 Tbl. butter into mixture. Season with salt and pepper. Add steamed mussels, shrimp, and scallops to soup. Heat well. Garnish bowls with chopped parsley. Serve.

Note:
From Trotters Restaurant, Atlanta. To steam mussels, place in large skillet with 1 inch water. Simmer until shells open.

꙳ Chris' Chili (page 36)

Asparagus in Vinaigrette (page 48)

Charleston Crab Stew

Ingredients for 4 servings:
2 Tbl. butter
½ cup green onions, minced
2 cloves garlic, minced
1 lb. crab meat, cooked and flaked
2 egg yolks
salt, to taste
white pepper, to taste
dash paprika
dash cayenne pepper
1 Tbl. parsley, minced
2 cups warm milk
1½ cups half-and-half
4 Tbl. dry sherry

Directions:
Melt butter in top part of double boiler over rapidly boiling water. Stir in onion and garlic. Sauté 2 minutes, until soft. Add crab meat. Whisk yolks in small bowl with salt, pepper, paprika, cayenne, and parsley. Blend yolk mixture into crab meat mixture slowly. Add warm milk and half-and-half. Stir constantly. Reduce heat. Cook about 15 minutes, or until thickened. Add sherry. Cook 1 minute more. Serve at once.

Note:
This soup is rich; it is a nice beginning to an elegant meal. It also can be served in punch cups at a buffet; then the recipe serves 6 to 8.

Pimiento Soup

Ingredients for 4 servings:
2 Tbl. butter
2 Tbl. onion, minced
2 Tbl. flour
2½ cups chicken stock
1 4-oz. jar chopped pimientos, drained
1 cup sour cream
salt, to taste
white pepper, to taste
sour cream, for garnish
pimientos, for garnish

Directions:
In large saucepan or stockpot, melt butter. Add onions. Sauté until soft, about 3 minutes. Add flour, whisking and cooking until thickened, 3 minutes more. Add stock all at once. Whisk until smooth. Let cool slightly. Add pimientos and stock mixture to bowl of food processor. Purée in batches with plastic blade. Turn purée into mixing bowl. Add sour cream. Salt and pepper to taste. Overseason soup, since it will be served cold. Chill well. Serve each portion with additional dollop of sour cream and chopped pimientos on top, for garnish.

Note:
From Kay Goldstein at Proof of the Pudding gourmet shop in Atlanta.

Peanut Soup

Ingredients for 6 servings:
2 Tbl. onion, minced
½ cup celery, thinly sliced
2 Tbl. butter
2 Tbl. flour
1 quart chicken broth
⅓ cup peanut butter
¼ tsp. salt
2 tsp. lemon juice
2 Tbl. dry sherry
1 cup half-and-half
2 Tbl. peanuts, chopped and roasted, for
    garnish

Directions:
Sauté onion and celery in butter until limp.
Stir in flour. Add chicken broth. Simmer
15-20 minutes. Strain. Stir broth into peanut
butter. Add salt and lemon juice. Stir in
sherry. Add half-and-half. Heat well. Serve
in hot cups garnished with chopped peanuts.

Note:
    If you don't serve this soup at once,
remove from heat after adding lemon juice.
Reheat just before serving and add sherry
and half-and-half.

Springtime Potato Soup

Ingredients for 4 to 6 servings:
1 Tbl. butter
1 leek, chopped
1 onion, chopped
4 cups chicken broth
2 cups potatoes, peeled and chopped
2 medium carrots, pared and sliced
8 spears fresh asparagus, sliced into
    ½-inch diagonals
3 cups fresh spinach, finely shredded
salt, to taste
black pepper, to taste

Directions:
In soup pot, melt butter. Add leek and
onion. Cook over low heat, covered, for 5
minutes. Add broth, potatoes, carrots, and
asparagus. Simmer, covered, 20 minutes.
Add spinach, salt, and pepper. Heat just
until spinach has wilted.

Note:
    This is a simple, refreshing soup for
springtime, when asparagus comes into
market.

Carrot Vichyssoise

Ingredients for 4 servings:
2 leeks, washed, drained, and sliced
 crosswise
4 Tbl. butter
4 cups chicken stock
3 medium potatoes, peeled and diced
3 large carrots, chopped
1 cup half-and-half
salt, to taste
white pepper, to taste
dash nutmeg
chives, chopped, for garnish

Directions:
In soup pot, sauté leeks in butter until soft, about 4 minutes. Add stock, potatoes, and carrots. Simmer about 30 minutes, or until vegetables are tender. In batches, purée mixture in blender or food processor. Return to pan. Before serving, heat. Add remaining ingredients. Don't let boil. Garnish with chives.

Note:
 This is brilliantly colored, and tastes especially good with beef.

Summer Squash Soup

Ingredients for 6 servings:
4 cups yellow crookneck squash, chopped
6 cups chicken stock
1 Tbl. butter
1 Tbl. oil
3 large carrots, chopped
3 medium onions, chopped
6 fresh tomatoes, peeled, seeded, and
 chopped
½ cup Parmesan cheese, grated
1 cup plain, low-fat yogurt
½ tsp. dried thyme *or* dried basil
salt, to taste
black pepper, freshly ground, to taste

Directions:
Place squash and stock in soup pot. Cook over medium heat until tender, about 15 minutes. In separate pan, sauté onions and carrots in butter and oil until soft, about 5 minutes. Add onions, carrots, and tomatoes to stockpot. Stir to combine. Cook 2 minutes more. Purée mixture in batches in food processor or blender. Return to pot. Add remaining ingredients. Heat slightly. Serve.

Chilled Cucumber Soup

Ingredients for 6 servings:
2 large cucumbers, peeled, seeded, and
    finely chopped
¼ cup onions, minced
1 tsp. garlic, minced
1 Tbl. olive oil
1 Tbl. red wine vinegar
3 cups plain, low-fat yogurt
1 cup sour cream
2 Tbl. fresh mint, minced
1 cup fresh *or* canned chicken stock
salt, to taste
pepper, to taste
cucumber slivers *or* fresh mint sprigs, for
    garnish

Directions:
Combine all ingredients in mixing bowl.
Chill 2-4 hours before serving. Serve with
either a thin sliver of cucumber on top or a
sprig of fresh mint.

Note:
    From Proof of the Pudding, Atlanta,
Georgia.

Cream of Asparagus Soup

Ingredients for 6 servings:
1 lb. fresh asparagus, tough edges
    trimmed, and cut into 1-inch pieces
1 cup chicken stock
¼ cup butter
¼ cup flour
2½ cups chicken stock
⅓ cup light cream
¼ tsp. black pepper
lemon wedges, for garnish

Directions:
Cook asparagus in 1 cup of stock until
tender. Melt butter in deep saucepan.
Remove from heat. Stir in flour. Add 2½
cups stock, a little at a time. Cook, stirring,
until slightly thickened. Stir in cream,
pepper, and cooked asparagus with liquid.
Heat through. Serve hot with lemon wedges
to squeeze over top of soup.

Seafood Gumbo

Ingredients for 10 to 12 servings:
4 Tbl. butter
4 Tbl. flour
2 Tbl. butter
3 medium-sized onions, chopped
5 cloves garlic, minced
¼ lb. ham, diced
12 pods okra, sliced
¼ tsp. thyme
2 bay leaves
2 Tbl. fresh parsley, minced
½ tsp. black pepper, freshly ground
salt, to taste
5 large fresh tomatoes, chopped *or* 2 cups
   chopped canned tomatoes
7 cups water
1 cup liquor reserved from oysters
1 lb. raw large shrimp, peeled and
   deveined
1 lb. crab meat
1 pint oysters, drained and liquor
   reserved
1 Tbl. filé

Directions:
Melt 4 Tbl. butter in large kettle or stockpot.
Add flour. Make a roux, by cooking and
stirring this constantly with a wooden spoon,
until the color turns from gold to dark red.
(Don't stop stirring for a second, or you will
scorch the roux!) When roux is red-colored,
remove from heat. Set aside. Melt 2 Tbl.
butter in skillet. Sauté chopped onions and
garlic until soft. Add ham. Stir and cook 2-3
minutes. Then add okra, stirring and cooking 2-3 minutes. Add thyme, bay leaves,
parsley, pepper, salt, tomatoes, water, and
liquor. Bring to boil. Reduce heat. Simmer
15 minutes. Add this entire mixture to roux
in kettle. Bring to boil again. Reduce heat to
gentle boil. Stirring constantly, cook 1 hour.
Add shrimp and crab meat. Cook 2 minutes.
Stir. Add oysters. Cook 1 minute more. Add
filé at very last. Stir well. Serve with crusty
garlic bread.

Note:
   This is the simplest, freshest gumbo
recipe I have found. It is not heavy, not
greasy, and glorifies the luscious crab,
shrimp, and oysters for which you have paid
so dearly.

Strawberry Soup

Ingredients for 6 servings:
1 quart ripe strawberries, hulled and
   rinsed
¾ cup sugar
pinch salt
1 cup sour cream
1 cup dry red wine
4 cups cold water
grated chocolate *or* fresh mint sprigs and
   sliced strawberries, for garnish

Directions:
In container of blender, combine strawberries, sugar, salt, sour cream, and wine. Purée 15 seconds, or until mixture is smooth. In large saucepan, combine purée with water. Heat soup slowly, stirring. Do not allow to boil. Chill at least 3 hours before serving. Serve garnished with grated chocolate for a dessert soup or fresh mint sprigs and sliced strawberries as an appetizer soup.

Note:
   The ruby color is magnificent. I prefer it cold as an appetizer, but some folks think it's sweet enough for dessert. Take your pick.

Bourbon Corn Chowder

Ingredients for 6 servings:
4 Tbl. unsalted butter
1 cup onion, chopped
2½ cups canned cream-style corn
¼ cup bourbon
¼ tsp. nutmeg
1 tsp. salt
black pepper, freshly ground, to taste
2-3 drops Tabasco sauce *or* ¼ tsp.
   crushed, dried red peppers
½ cup chicken stock
½ cup heavy cream

Directions:
Melt butter in 2½-quart saucepan. Add onion. Cook until transparent. Stir in corn. Heat bourbon in small pan. Take off heat. Ignite. Let bourbon flame 1 minute. Then pour over corn mixture, while still flaming. Stir in nutmeg, salt, pepper, Tabasco sauce, chicken stock, and cream. Heat through. Serve hot.

Note:
   This is a good accompaniment to grilled hamburgers in the summertime, or with hot, homemade bread and sausages in the wintertime.

Cranberry Relish

Ingredients for about 6 cups:
3 tart apples, peeled and chopped
2 oranges, cut into fourths
3 cups cranberries
1 cup sugar
⅛ tsp. salt
1 cup pecans, finely chopped

Directions:
Combine apples, oranges, and cranberries. Run mixture through grinder. Transfer to mixing bowl. Add sugar, salt, and pecans. Blend well.

Note:
You don't peel the oranges in this recipe from Ernestine McHarry of Athens, Tennessee. That's what gives this relish its distinctive tart flavor — a wonderful partner to turkey and dressing.

Tuna Bean Salad

Ingredients for 8 to 10 servings:
½ lb. dried white beans
water
1 cup olive oil
⅓ cup lemon juice
¼ tsp. Tabasco sauce
2 green onions, chopped
2 Tbl. parsley, chopped
1 6½-7 oz. can tuna, drained
1 large tomato, chopped
2 hard-cooked eggs, peeled and chopped
¼ cup chopped, pitted black olives
salt, to taste
black pepper, to taste
¼ tsp. crushed red peppers
½ tsp. ground rosemary

Directions:
Soak beans with water to cover overnight. Next day, drain beans. Place in kettle with enough water to cover. Bring beans to boil for 2 minutes. Cover. Simmer about 1½ hours or until beans are done but not soft. Add more water during cooking as needed to keep beans from sticking to pot.
Drain beans. Let cool 5 minutes. Turn into large mixing bowl. Add remaining ingredients. Mix well. Chill before serving.

Note:
This recipe is a summer favorite. It comes from Proof of the Pudding in Atlanta.

Asparagus in Vinaigrette

Ingredients for 4 servings:
1 lb. fresh asparagus
salted water
½ cup vegetable oil
2 Tbl. lemon juice
1 Tbl. green onions, chopped
1 tsp. Dijon mustard
1 clove garlic, crushed
¼-½ tsp. dried tarragon, crushed
⅛ tsp. salt

Directions:
Wash asparagus. Break off tough end. Cook whole in skillet with 1 inch boiling, salted water until crisp-tender, about 8 minutes. Drain. Place in shallow glass dish. In small bowl, combine remaining ingredients, whisking to combine. Pour over asparagus. Cover. Chill overnight.

Note:
    Drain before serving. The leftover marinade can be saved and used as a salad dressing.

Tennessee Cole Slaw

Ingredients for 8 to 10 servings:
¾ cup sugar
¼ cup vegetable oil
¼ cup cider vinegar
1 Tbl. salt
1 tsp. black pepper, coarsely ground
1 Tbl. dry mustard
1 tsp. celery seed
1 green pepper, seeded and sliced
3 lbs. cabbage, shredded
2 medium-sized onions, sliced

Directions:
In saucepan, combine sugar, oil, vinegar, salt, pepper, mustard, and celery seed. Bring to boil. Turn off heat. Stir well. Layer pepper, cabbage, and onion in glass bowl. Pour dressing over all. Cover. Refrigerate 24 hours before serving.

Note:
    This recipe is ideal for those of you who don't like mayonnaise in cole slaw.

Oriental Asparagus Salad

Ingredients for 6 servings:
2 lbs. fresh asparagus spears
1 10¾-oz. can beef *or* chicken consommé
2 Tbl. soy sauce
½ cup dry sherry
½ cup vegetable oil
¼ tsp. ground ginger
lettuce
3 hard-cooked eggs, sliced, to garnish
  (optional)
paprika, as garnish
marinade reserved from asparagus, as
  garnish (optional)

Directions:
Wash and trim asparagus, breaking off each stalk as far down as it is tender. Steam in consommé in large skillet about 5 minutes, or until just tender. Drain and cool. Meanwhile, combine soy sauce, sherry, oil, and ginger. Pour over cooked asparagus. Chill several hours. When ready to serve, drain asparagus. Place several spears on lettuce. Top each serving with 3 slices of hard-cooked egg, if desired. Sprinkle with paprika. Serve with additional marinade, if desired.

Note:
   Serve with any kind of chicken dish — roasted, grilled, or fried.

Mango-Orange Salad

Ingredients for 4 servings:
3 medium mangoes, peeled and diced
4 oranges, peeled and cut into segments
2 bunches watercress, trimmed of stalks
2 Tbl. green onions, chopped
Curry Dressing (see page 191)
¼ cup sunflower seeds

Directions:
In large salad bowl, combine mangoes, oranges, watercress, and green onion. Prepare salad dressing. Pour dressing over salad. Toss to coat. Garnish with sunflower seeds.

Note:
   Serve with shrimp, Cuban chicken, or any spicy dish. The mangoes will cool the fire.

Cold Curried Rice Salad

Ingredients for 10 servings:
2 8-oz. packages chicken-flavored
  Rice-a-Roni
8 green onions, sliced
1 green pepper, chopped
2 6-oz. jars marinated artichoke hearts,
  chopped, liquid reserved
¼ cup toasted almonds, sliced
½ cup green olives, sliced
2 tsp. curry powder
⅔ cup mayonnaise
liquid reserved from artichokes

Directions:
Cook rice as packages direct, using oil, rather than butter. Refrigerate. Add remaining ingredients, except mayonnaise and curry powder. Mix mayonnaise and curry powder. Add to rice mixture. Blend in artichoke liquid. Stir. Chill. This keeps for several days, and is delicious with chili or grilled chicken.

Note:
    From accomplished Atlanta cook Anita Kidd, whose recipe files 'most any cook would love to steal.

Black-Eyed Pea Vinaigrette

Ingredients for 6 to 8 servings:
2 1-lb. cans black-eyed peas
1 small onion, minced
2 red bell peppers, diced
¼ cup fresh parsley, minced
½ tsp. dried dill weed *or* 1½ tsp. fresh
  dill, minced
¼ cup olive oil
¼ cup red wine vinegar
salt, to taste
pepper, to taste

Directions:
Rinse and drain peas. Combine in mixing bowl with onion, peppers, parsley, and dill. Sprinkle with equal amounts of oil and vinegar, until well moistened. Salt and pepper to taste. Marinate in refrigerator for several hours.

Note:
    This dish is perfect for New Year's Day when you're serving Yankees who claim they don't like black-eyed peas. It is also great for summer picnics with sliced ham, or for fall pig roasts.

Vidalia Onion-Tomato Salad

Ingredients for 6 servings:
1 jumbo Vidalia onion, thinly sliced and separated into rings
4 tomatoes, peeled and sliced
2 Tbl. fresh herbs, chopped and mixed (parsley, chives, basil, and dill)
celery salt, to taste
black pepper, freshly ground, to taste

Directions:
On the bottom of large bowl or serving platter, spread onion rings. Cover with single layer of tomato slices. Sprinkle herbs, celery salt, and pepper over all. Cover. Refrigerate at least 3 hours. You can serve a vinaigrette dressing with this, but you don't need to.

Note:
This recipe is a salute to our sweet Georgia onions.

Pasta Primavera Salad

Ingredients for 6 servings:
2 medium zucchini squash, sliced
2 small summer squash, sliced
2 medium carrots, peeled and chopped
¼ medium purple onion, minced
¾ lb. fresh pasta (fettuccine, linguine, or shells), cooked to *al dente,* drained
Primavera Dressing (see page 194)

Directions:
Toss zucchini squash, summer squash, carrots, and onion with pasta. Prepare dressing. Pour over all. Toss to mix. Cover and chill until serving time.

Note:
From Janet Thomizer of the Pasta and Cheese Shop in Lenox Square, Atlanta, Georgia.

Taco Salad

Ingredients for 4 servings:
1 lb. ground beef
1 1½-oz. package taco seasoning *or* 2
   Tbl. chili powder
¾ cup water
1 tsp. cumin seeds
1 head iceberg lettuce, shredded
2 tomatoes, diced
1 15-oz. can kidney beans, drained
1 medium avocado, peeled and sliced
6 green onions, chopped
½ lb. Cheddar *or* Monterey jack cheese,
   shredded
1 cup corn chips, crumbled
hot tomato salsa *or* green chile salsa, for
   garnish (optional)

Directions:
Brown beef in skillet. Drain. Add taco
seasoning and water. Simmer 10 minutes.
Add cumin seeds. Layer salad in glass bowl.
Start with lettuce, then tomatoes, beans,
avocado, onions, and cheese. Top with hot
meat mixture and crumbled corn chips. Best
with hot tomato salsa or green chile salsa to
crown the salad.

Broccoli-Pasta Salad

Ingredients for 12 servings:
2 lbs. fresh angel hair pasta
salted water
¼ cup olive oil
2 bunches green onions, chopped
2 bunches broccoli, chopped (reserve
   ends of stalks for soup)
6 cloves garlic, minced
1 Tbl. fresh oregano, minced *or* 1 tsp.
   dried oregano
1 Tbl. fresh basil, minced *or* 1 tsp. dried
   basil
½ cup olive oil
¼ cup red wine vinegar
1 cup black olives, chopped
3 tomatoes, peeled, seeded, and diced
salt, to taste
black pepper, to taste

Directions:
Cook pasta in boiling salted water until
done, but still firm, about 4 minutes. Drain.
Rinse with cold water. Drain. Add ¼ cup
olive oil to pasta. Toss. Let cool. When cool,
place pasta in large serving bowl with
remaining ingredients. Cover. Chill. Allow
to marinate in refrigerator 3 hours. Top with
freshly grated Parmesan cheese, if desired.

Note:
   From the Colony Restaurant, Longboat
Key, Florida.

Sesame Noodle Salad

Ingredients for 6 to 8 servings:
1 lb. linguine, cooked, drained, and
  cooled
3 Tbl. soy sauce
¼ cup dark sesame oil
¼ tsp. black pepper, freshly ground
½ red bell pepper, seeded and chopped
¼ cup watercress, chopped
½ tsp. garlic, minced

Directions:
Mix linguine with soy sauce, sesame oil, and pepper. Lightly mix in red pepper, watercress, and garlic. Chill, until ready to serve. Delicious with any grilled or roasted meats, or with an impromptu stir-fry combination.

Note:
This recipe was served at a Food Editor's Conference with a medley of cold salads. It is from the American Café in Washington, D.C.

Skillet Salad

Ingredients for 12 servings:
4 lbs. green peppers, cut into halves
  lengthwise, cleaned, and cut into strips
10 onions, preferably Vidalia onions,
  peeled and sliced
6-8 Tbl. olive oil
12 ripe tomatoes, sliced
2 7-oz. jars whole pimientos, cut into
  ½-inch strips and drained
salt, to taste
black pepper, freshly ground, to taste

Directions:
Sauté peppers and onions in olive oil over moderate heat about 8 minutes, or until vegetables are slightly colored. Add remaining ingredients to pepper and onion mixture. Cook 4-5 minutes longer, until tomatoes are soft but not mushy. Serve hot with grilled chicken and garlic bread. You can serve this cold, too, for a picnic salad along with cold, sliced, rare beef, lamb, or chicken.

Note:
A totable salad, since it doesn't have to be kept cold and is better tasting at room temperature.

My Favorite Potato Salad

Ingredients for 8 servings:
8 cups unpeeled red-skinned potatoes,
    boiled and chunked (about 3 lbs.)
1 medium onion, chopped
2 cloves garlic, minced
2 Tbl. olive oil
2 Tbl. white wine vinegar
salt, to taste
pepper, to taste
dash red pepper
½ cup parsley, chopped
¼ cup chives, chopped
½ cup homemade Lemon Mayonnaise
    (see page 189)
½ cup plain, low-fat yogurt
black olives, sliced, as garnish

Directions:
Cut still-warm potatoes into chunks. Place in
mixing bowl with onion and garlic. Season
with olive oil, vinegar, salt, pepper, and red
pepper. Toss to coat. Cover. Refrigerate
until chilled. Mix in parsley and chives. Mix
together mayonnaise and yogurt. Add to
potato mixture. Toss to coat. Adjust seasonings. Place sliced olives on top as a
garnish.

Note:
    Two secrets to a good potato salad are
waxy potatoes, seasoned while still warm,
and a homemade mayonnaise. Unlike some
potato salads, this recipe is not sweet. I
believe cole slaw should be sweet, not potato
salad. This recipe was inspired by those
lovely potato salads you find made with all
sorts of homemade mayonnaises in the
markets of Paris.

Artichoke-Zucchini Salad

Ingredients for 6 servings:
3-4 small zucchini (¾ lb.)
⅓ cup green *or* red bell peppers, seeded and slivered
¼ cup green onion, chopped
1 Tbl. vegetable oil
¼ tsp. dried basil *or* 1 tsp. fresh basil, minced
¼ tsp. dried tarragon *or* 1 tsp. fresh tarragon, minced
dash white pepper
2 6-oz. jars marinated artichoke hearts, reserve marinade
butter lettuce *or* Boston lettuce

Ingredients for dressing:
marinade reserved from artichoke hearts
2 Tbl. oil
1 Tbl. white wine vinegar

Directions:
Grate zucchini to make 3 cups. Combine with pepper slivers and green onions. Mix together 1 Tbl. oil, basil, tarragon, and pepper. Pour over vegetables to coat. Toss. Chill. At serving time, drain artichokes; save marinade. Combine dressing ingredients. Stir. On each serving plate, place leaf of lettuce. Top with ½ cup zucchini mixture. Arrange drained artichokes to side. Pass dressing at table. Serve with fried, broiled, poached, or stir-fried chicken.

Note:
When the summer proliferation of zucchini arrives, try this.

Winter Potato Salad

Ingredients for 4 servings:
2 cups potatoes, peeled and diced
water
1 cup watercress leaves (no stalks), coarsely chopped
1 cup red cabbage, shredded
1 clove garlic, minced
3 Tbl. olive oil
rind of 1 lemon, grated
juice of 1 lemon
1 tsp. salt
¼ tsp. Dijon-style mustard
black pepper, freshly ground, to taste

Directions:
Cook potatoes in boiling water until tender, but not mushy — 5-10 minutes. Drain. Cool. Toss potatoes with watercress and cabbage. In small bowl, combine remaining ingredients. Pour over vegetables. Toss to coat.

Note:
Hearty. Serve with pork, marinated beef, or sausages.

Overnight Layered Salad

Ingredients for 8 servings:
1 lb. fresh spinach, washed, drained, and
  torn into pieces
1 small head Boston lettuce, washed,
  drained, and torn into pieces
4 hard-cooked eggs, peeled and sliced
½ lb. bacon, cooked, drained, and
  crumbled
⅓ cup green onions, chopped
1 10-oz. package frozen green peas,
  thawed
1 8-oz. can sliced water chestnuts,
  drained
fresh parsley, chopped, for garnish
Parmesan cheese, freshly grated, for
  garnish

Ingredients for dressing:
1 4-oz. package ranch dressing mix
1 cup mayonnaise
1 cup plain, low-fat yogurt
½-1 cup sour cream

Directions:
Mix together all dressing ingredients. Layer
all salad ingredients (except parsley and
Parmesan cheese) in order in glass bowl.
Pour dressing over all. Top with parsley and
Parmesan cheese.

Note:
     This is a standard New Year's Day salad
to serve with country ham and biscuits and
black-eyed peas. Spinach symbolizes money
in the coming year. This salad improves with
storage, and should be made the night or day
before serving.

Chicken Salad with Basil

Ingredients for 4 servings:
2 cups fresh basil leaves
¾ cup olive oil
2 Tbl. pine nuts *or* walnuts, chopped
2 cloves garlic, crushed
1 tsp. salt
6 Tbl. Parmesan cheese, freshly grated
1 lb. boneless chicken breasts, cooked
    and cubed, cooled to room temperature
10 pitted black olives, sliced
lettuce
2 Tbl. Parmesan cheese, freshly grated
black pepper, freshly ground

Directions:
In food processor or blender container, finely mince basil. Add olive oil, nuts, garlic, and salt. Blend well. Pour into mixing bowl. Stir in 6 Tbl. Parmesan cheese. Toss with chicken and olives. Line 4 salad plates with lettuce. Mound salad on top. Sprinkle each with Parmesan cheese and black pepper.

Old-Fashioned Chicken Salad

Ingredients for 8 servings:
1 3½-4 lb. broiler-fryer chicken
water, to cover
½ cup vegetable oil
2 Tbl. white wine vinegar
1 tsp. Dijon mustard
½ tsp. salt
½ tsp. black pepper, freshly ground
3 ribs celery, diced
½ cup mayonnaise, or to taste
1 Tbl. small capers (optional)
salt, to taste
black pepper, to taste

Directions:
Simmer chicken, covered, in enough water to cover 3-4 hours, or until just done. As soon as chicken is cool enough to handle, remove bones and skin, keeping meat in large pieces. Combine oil, vinegar, mustard, salt, and pepper. Pour over chicken meat. Marinate, covered, in refrigerator, until well chilled. When cold, cube chicken. Combine meat with remaining ingredients. Season with salt and pepper. Chill until served.

Note:
For variation, add chopped fresh dill or tarragon, sliced black olives, sliced hard-cooked eggs, thawed frozen green peas, or chopped green onion.

Wild Rice and Chicken Salad

Ingredients for 4 to 6 servings:
3 cups water
1 cup wild rice, rinsed
2 green onions, minced
3 hard-cooked eggs, chopped
2 cups chicken, cooked and diced *or* 12
  oz. cooked shrimp
tomatoes, sliced, to garnish
avocado, sliced, to garnish

Ingredients for Tarragon Dressing:
1 cup mayonnaise
¼ cup white wine vinegar
½ tsp. dry mustard
2 Tbl. Dijon-style mustard
2 Tbl. sugar
½ tsp. dried tarragon, crushed
salt, to taste
pepper, to taste

Directions:
Combine all dressing ingredients in small
bowl. Stir well.
    Bring water to boil in medium saucepan.
Stir in rice. Reduce heat. Cover. Simmer
about 40 minutes, or until rice is fluffy. (You
may need to open the lid during cooking to
let some of the water evaporate.) Toss
together rice, onions, eggs, and chicken in
mixing bowl with enough dressing to moist-
en. Garnish salad with tomato and avocado.
Serve additional dressing with salad at table.

Note:
    Try with shrimp or crab meat.

Curried Rice and Shrimp Salad

Ingredients for 8 to 10 servings:
2 lbs. medium shrimp, boiled, peeled,
  and deveined
½ cup Mustard Vinaigrette dressing (see
  page 186)
4 cups water
1 tsp. salt
2 cups raw long-grain rice
½ cup vinaigrette dressing
¾ cup mayonnaise
3 Tbl. onion, minced
2 Tbl. curry powder
1 Tbl. Dijon-style mustard
salt, to taste
white pepper, to taste
hard-cooked egg slices, as garnish
parsley, chopped, to garnish

Directions:
Marinate shrimp in ½ cup Mustard vinaigrette dressing 30 minutes, or while cooking
rice. Bring 4 cups water and 1 tsp. salt to boil
in saucepan. Stir in rice. Cover. Steam 20
minutes or until fluffy. In mixing bowl, toss
cooked rice with shrimp, ½ cup Mustard
Vinaigrette dressing, mayonnaise, onion,
curry powder, and mustard. Season with salt
and pepper. Chill. Serve on bed of lettuce.
Garnish with hard-cooked egg slices and
chopped parsley.

Note:
    From Atlanta cooking instructor Peggy
Foreman.

Green Bean Salad with Mustard Dressing

Ingredients for 4 servings:
water
1½ lbs. tender green beans, stems
  removed
2 tsp. salt
2 Tbl. stone-ground mustard with
  horseradish
6 Tbl. olive oil
2 Tbl. white wine vinegar
2 Tbl. fresh chives, minced
4 large lettuce leaves

Directions:
Bring 2-quart saucepan of water to boil. Add beans and salt. Cook until tender; start checking after 5 minutes. Drain beans. Rinse under cold water. Cool. Place mustard in large bowl. Whisk in olive oil, vinegar, and chives. Fold in beans. Toss to combine. Spoon beans onto lettuce leaves.

Note:
  Plochman's mustard is best here.

Oriental Cucumbers

Ingredients for 6 to 8 servings:
1 cup sesame oil
2 Tbl. soy sauce
2 Tbl. white vinegar
½ tsp. salt
2 cloves garlic, minced
1 tsp. ginger root, grated
1 tsp. crushed red pepper
5-6 medium cucumbers, peeled and
  seeded

Directions:
Combine all ingredients, except cucumber. Quarter cucumbers. Cut quarters into eighths. Place cucumbers in glass dish. Pour dressing over all. Cover with plastic wrap. Marinate in refrigerator at least 1 hour.

Note:
  The sesame oil imparts an Oriental taste to a standard Southern garden item.

Eggs & Cheese

The Place For Boiled Custard

I always think of boiled custard along with fruitcake and other holiday goodies, but some Southerners have prepared the thin custard for its medicinal qualities. The custard, they say, soothes a weak stomach and even can mend a broken heart. Sweetened a tad with sugar and often spiked with vanilla, boiled custard was administered to "invalids" in the old days.

This custard fits the general description of a custard, a combination of eggs and milk which is cooked in a double boiler or in the oven.

To make a boiled or "soft" custard, combine 1 egg for a thin custard or 2 for a heavier, richer blend with 1 tablespoon sugar and a dash of salt in the upper portion of a double boiler. Slowly add 1 cup scalded milk and stir and heat over simmering water until the mixture coats a spoon. A ½ teaspoon of vanilla or grating of nutmeg is added before the custard is cooled.

Boiled custard is either served in punch cups or mixed with fresh fruit. The only secret to making a proper boiled custard is no secret at all: Begin with fresh milk and fresh eggs.

From the basic custard, you can create more than just a drink. Pour it into the bottom of a glass serving dish, cover with a light spongecake, douse the cake with sherry, and top with whipped cream or more custard. Or, by pouring boiled custard over meringues cooked in hot milk, you can create floating islands.

Boiled custard isn't just holiday fare; it can and should be served frequently. It's a true part of our Southern heritage.

Overnight Cheese Soufflé

Ingredients for 6 servings:
4 Tbl. butter
6 Tbl. flour
1 cup evaporated milk
1 cup sharp Cheddar *or* Swiss cheese,
  shredded
6 egg yolks, well beaten
1 tsp. salt
6 egg whites

Directions:
Grease 2-quart soufflé dish. Make 3-inch foil
collar to fit around top edge. Grease inside
of collar. Secure with piece of kitchen twine
tied around upper edge of dish.

Melt butter in 2-quart saucepan. Whisk
in flour, until smooth. Stir in milk slowly,
whisking until mixture is thick. Take off
heat. Add cheese, egg yolks, and salt.
Return to heat. Cook on low, until cheese
has melted and mixture is smooth. Let cool
30 minutes.

Meanwhile, beat egg whites in separate
bowl, until stiff peaks form. Fold whites into
cooled base mixture. Pour into prepared
soufflé dish. Cover top lightly with plastic
wrap. Place in refrigerator overnight.

The next morning, or right before guests
at brunch are ready to eat, preheat oven to
350°. Place soufflé in oven 35-45 minutes, or
until soufflé has puffed and top is golden.
Remove collar and serve at once.

Note:
Contrary to the general opinion that
soufflés must go directly into the oven after
egg whites are folded in, they can be
prepared the day before and refrigerated
overnight. You suffer no real loss in volume.

Broccoli Soufflé

Ingredients for 4 servings:
2 cups broccoli, chopped *or* 1 10-oz.
   package frozen broccoli
2 Tbl. butter
2 Tbl. flour
½ tsp. salt
½ cup milk
4 egg yolks
¼ cup Parmesan cheese, grated
4 egg whites

Directions:
Preheat oven to 350°. In covered saucepan cook fresh broccoli 8-10 minutes. Cook frozen broccoli according to package directions. Drain well. Chop up any large pieces. Melt butter in medium saucepan. Whisk in flour and salt. Add milk. Cook and stir until bubbling. Remove from heat. Beat egg yolks until thick and lemon-colored. Slowly stir half hot mixture into yolks. Return to hot mixture. Stir well. Blend in cheese and broccoli. In separate bowl, beat egg whites, until stiff peaks form. Fold into broccoli mixture. Turn into ungreased 1-quart soufflé dish. Bake 35-40 minutes. Serve at once.

Note:
   Serve this with any simple chicken or fish dish.

Welsh Rabbit

Ingredients for 2 servings:
½ lb. raw milk Cheddar cheese,
   extra-sharp
1 tsp. dry mustard
1 tsp. paprika
⅛ tsp. cayenne pepper
nutmeg, to taste (optional)
½ cup warm beer
1 Tbl. butter
1 egg, beaten
salt, to taste
dry toast, sliced tomatoes, and crisp
   bacon slices

Directions:
Shred cheese. Set aside. Place mustard, paprika, cayenne pepper, and nutmeg in small bowl. Add beer a little at a time, to make paste. Melt butter in top of double boiler. Add paste. When mixture is hot, add cheese. Stir with wooden spoon, until cheese melts. Add egg, stirring until smooth. Don't let boil. Season with salt. Serve atop dry toast, tomato slices, and bacon slices.

Note:
   From an article on cooking with beer. In this recipe, beer provides the flavor.

Zucchini-Cheese Soufflé

Ingredients for 4 servings:
½ lb. zucchini, shredded
¼ tsp. salt
2 Tbl. Parmesan cheese, grated
3 Tbl. unsalted butter
3 Tbl. flour
¾ cup milk, scalded
¼ cup onion, minced
2 Tbl. unsalted butter
½ cup Swiss cheese, shredded
¼ cup Parmesan cheese, grated
dash nutmeg
salt, to taste
pepper, to taste
5 egg whites
1 Tbl. Parmesan cheese, grated

Directions:
In colander, toss zucchini with ¼ tsp. salt. Let stand 30 minutes. Squeeze zucchini in towel, removing as much water as possible. Fit well buttered, 1-quart soufflé dish with buttered foil collar. Sprinkle both with 2 Tbl. Parmesan cheese. (Individual soufflé dishes may also be used.)

Preheat oven to 375°. In saucepan, melt 3 Tbl. butter over medium-low heat. Stir in flour. Cook, stirring, until thick. Remove from heat. Add milk. Whisk until thick and smooth. Transfer to large bowl. In sauté pan, cook onion in 2 Tbl. butter 2 minutes. Add zucchini. Cook 2 minutes. Add to sauce, along with Swiss cheese, ¼ cup Parmesan cheese, nutmeg, salt, and pepper. Beat egg whites until stiff. Fold into zucchini mixture. Pour into soufflé dish. Top with 1 Tbl. Parmesan cheese. Bake 30 minutes.

Note:
This divine recipe comes from Anita Kidd of Atlanta.

Vidalia Onion Custard

Ingredients for 4 servings:
2 lbs. Vidalia onions, thinly sliced
3 Tbl. butter
1 cup milk
2 eggs
1 egg yolk
1 tsp. salt
¼ tsp. nutmeg
white pepper, to taste

Directions:
Preheat oven to 325°. In large skillet, cook onions in butter over medium heat until soft, about 20 minutes. Let cool. In large bowl, whisk together remaining ingredients. Beat mixture until well combined. Stir in onions. Transfer mixture to well buttered, 2-quart baking dish. Bake 40-50 minutes, or until lightly golden and skewer inserted in center comes out clean. Serve hot or at room temperature.

Note:
    This dish is delicious with beef.

One Skillet Breakfast

Ingredients for 3 to 4 servings:
6 slices bacon, diced
3 Tbl. drippings reserved from bacon
1 small green pepper, seeded and diced
2 Tbl. onion, diced
3 medium-sized potatoes, cooked, peeled, and diced
½ cup Cheddar cheese, shredded
6 eggs, lightly beaten
salt, to taste
black pepper, to taste

Directions:
In large skillet, sauté bacon until crisp. Remove with slotted spatula. Drain on paper towels. Crumble. Reserve 3 Tbl. drippings. To hot drippings, add green pepper, onion, and potatoes. Cook over medium heat, stirring constantly, until potatoes are golden. Sprinkle cheese over mixture. Stir, until cheese melts. Pour eggs into skillet. Season with salt and pepper. Cook over low heat, stirring, until eggs set. Scatter crumbled bacon on top of mixture and serve.

Creamed Eggs

Ingredients for 6 servings:
6 hard-cooked eggs, peeled, and cut into
   ¼-inch thick slices
4 Tbl. butter
4 Tbl. flour
2 cups milk, scalded
1 Tbl. green onion, minced
½ tsp. dried thyme
1 Tbl. Dijon-style mustard

Directions:
Prepare eggs. Set aside. In small saucepan, melt butter over medium heat. Add flour. Whisk until smooth. Add milk all at once. Whisk until mixture has thickened. Add green onion, thyme, and mustard. Stir well. Heat through. Gently add eggs. Cook about 3 minutes, or until egg slices are heated. Serve over toast points or over buttered, broiled biscuits.

Note:
   This is a great alternative to egg salad for using up leftover, hard-cooked eggs from Easter.

Homegrown Tomato Pie

Ingredients for 6 servings:
pastry for 9-inch pie shell
2 medum-sized, ripe tomatoes
1 lb. ground chuck
½ cup onion, chopped
1 tsp. dried oregano, crumbled
1 tsp. salt
¼ tsp. black pepper, freshly ground
4 eggs, lightly beaten
1¼ cups milk, scalded
2 Tbl. dry bread crumbs

Directions:
Preheat oven to 375°. Place pastry in 9-inch pie pan. Prick bottom and sides with fork. Bake 10 minutes. Remove from oven. Set aside.
   Core tomatoes. Cut into ¼-inch slices. Cut each slice into halves. Set aside. In large skillet, brown chuck and onion 5 minutes. Drain off fat. Add oregano, salt, and black pepper. Cook and stir 2 minutes. Remove from heat.
   In medium bowl, beat eggs with milk. Stir in meat mixture. Mix well. Sprinkle bread crumbs over crust. Arrange half tomato slices over crumbs. Pour egg mixture into shell. Bake 20 minutes. Arrange remaining tomato slices over top in overlapping pattern. Bake until custard sets, about 10 minutes more.

Note:
   This hearty dish provides a welcome change of pace from quiche.

Eggs in Purgatory

Ingredients for 6 servings:
5 medium mushrooms, sliced
2 Tbl. butter
3 medium-sized onions, chopped
2 Tbl. butter
1 35-oz. can peeled Italian tomatoes,
   undrained
4 Tbl. butter
2 tsp. dried basil
2 tsp. dried oregano
salt, to taste
black pepper, to taste
1 6-oz. can tomato paste (optional)
6 eggs

Directions:
Sauté mushrooms in 2 Tbl. butter, until golden. Reserve. Sauté onion in another 2 Tbl. butter, until soft. Return mushrooms to skillet. Add tomatoes (undrained), 4 Tbl. butter, basil, oregano, salt, and pepper. Simmer, uncovered, 1 hour. If mixture is thin, add tomato paste. In small skillet, place 6 cups tomato mixture. Heat to just below boiling. Crack eggs. Place in depressions made with spoon in tomato mixture. Cover. Cook just 4-5 minutes. Remove eggs to plate with spatula. Allow equal amounts of sauce around each egg. Serve with sausage and toasted biscuits, or French bread.

Note:
   This makes an excellent Sunday supper when served with a tossed green salad. It's also a good brunch dish.

Fish & Shellfish

Roasting Oysters

The 1800s sometimes have been called the oyster century, when our country's craze with oysters led us to savor the mollusks on the half shell, in pies, scalloped in casseroles, creamed in patty shells, dished up in stews for Sunday supper, and roasted at one of the South's best outdoor feasts — the oyster "bake."

Along the coasts of North Carolina, South Carolina, Georgia, and Mississippi, uncultivated, or "wild," oysters were dug from local streams, washed, scrubbed, and then shoveled onto sheet metal atop crackling fires. Wet croker sacks were applied to the top of oysters to create steam. When the oysters popped, they were served up at once to diners, usually with plenty of melted butter for dipping.

In the plantation days, oyster roasts highlighted political gatherings. Oysters were served soon after the men's whiskey punch and the women's eggnog glasses had run dry, and the party-goers were ready to feast. And they usually were the forerunner to a larger, more elaborate meal to follow.

Today, roasted wild oysters are such a delicacy to track down that they're a meal in themselves. You still can find local restaurants, such as Teeple's Seafood in Thunderbolt, Georgia, outside Savannah, serving the oysters with butter and barbecue sauce. And many Southerners along the coast still stage oyster roasts in the spring, much like those of us to the north roast a pig on the spit each fall.

These wild, uncultivated oysters, unlike the large, cultivated Gulf oysters, must be roasted to be eaten, because even if you've got a crowbar and a hammer in hand, you can't crack their cement-like shells to eat them raw. The oysters grow in a honeycomb-fashion. They are smaller than Gulf oysters, but because of their freshness and their rarity, they taste ever so much better.

Scallops with Peppers

Ingredients for 4 servings:
2 lbs. bay scallops, well cleaned
salt, to taste
black pepper, to taste
2 Tbl. olive oil
2 Tbl. butter, divided
¾ cup green bell peppers, cleaned,
  seeded, and cut into julienne strips
¾ cup red bell peppers, cleaned, seeded,
  and cut into julienne strips
1 clove garlic, minced
¼ cup capers, drained
½ cup fresh bread crumbs
¼ cup white wine
2 Tbl. butter

Directions:
Preheat broiler. Sprinkle scallops with salt
and pepper. Heat oil over range in large,
heavy skillet. Add scallops. Cook over very
high heat, stirring, about 2 minutes. Transfer
scallops to baking dish that will hold them in
one layer. Set aside.

To skillet, add 2 Tbl. butter. When hot,
add pepper strips and garlic. Cook, stirring,
until soft, about 1 minute. Add capers. Stir.
Add bread crumbs and wine. Heat well.
Spoon mixture over scallops. Dot with
remaining 2 Tbl. butter. Place under broiler.
Cook about 4 minutes.

Note:
The peppers make the dish most color-
ful, but it's more spectacular when half the
sweet red peppers are orange-red and the
others vivid dark red.

Scallops and Fettuccine

Ingredients for 4 servings as the main course or 8 servings as the first course:
4 quarts water
1 lb. fresh *or* dried spinach fettuccine
½ cup flour
salt, to taste
black pepper, to taste
1 lb. fresh bay *or* sea scallops, well washed
4 Tbl. butter
salt, to taste
pepper, to taste
½ tsp. crushed red pepper
4 Tbl. butter
Parmesan cheese, grated

Directions:
Bring water to full boil in large pot. Add fettuccine. Cook at slow boil, until noodles are just tender, about 5 minutes or less, depending on your pasta. Meanwhile, combine flour with salt and pepper and roll scallops in mixture. Shake off excess. Melt 4 Tbl. butter in skillet. Add scallops in single layer. Sauté briefly, shaking pan to cook on all sides. Add salt, pepper, and red pepper. Scallops will cook in less than 5 minutes if bay scallops, longer if sea scallops.

When fettuccine is done, drain and toss with 4 Tbl. butter. Season to taste. Spoon into serving bowl or onto serving plates. Top noodles with scallops. Serve with grated Parmesan cheese.

Note:
If using sea scallops, cut them into halves to cut down cooking time and for a prettier presentation.

Broiled Swordfish Steaks with Onions

Ingredients for 6 servings:
6 6-8-oz. swordfish steaks, about 1 inch
  thick
salt, to taste
black pepper, to taste
½ cup vegetable oil
½ cup dry vermouth
juice of 2 lemons
½ tsp. dried oregano
½ tsp. dried basil
½ tsp. dried thyme
6 medium onions, peeled, sliced, and
  separated into rings
¼ cup vegetable oil
butter, melted

Directions:
Season steaks with salt and pepper. Combine ½ cup oil, vermouth, lemon juice, oregano, basil, and thyme in small bowl. Pour over fish. Marinate, covered and chilled, for 2 hours, turning once. Let come to room temperature before cooking. Meanwhile, fry onions in ¼ cup oil until translucent but crisp. Set aside.

Broil fish on both sides for a total cooking time of 9-10 minutes. Arrange steaks on platter, surrounded by onion rings. Brush melted butter over all.

Note:
Swordfish steaks are meaty enough to satisfy beef lovers, but are lower in fat and calories than beef.

Smoked Mullet

Ingredients for 6 servings:
1 lb. hickory chips
2 quarts water
charcoal briquets, burning
4 lbs. mullet, sliced lengthwise
1 cup salt
1 gallon water
1 3-oz. box crab boil seasoning
vegetable oil, for basting

Directions:
Cover hickory chips with 2 quarts water. Soak several hours in cool place. Cover charcoal briquets, which are turning slightly gray, with chips, to create smoke. Rinse fish. In large bowl combine salt, 1 gallon water, and crab seasoning. Add fish. Refrigerate 30 minutes, stirring occasionally. Remove fish from brine. Rinse. Pat dry. Place fish, skin side down, on well-greased grill, about 4-6 inches from smoking coals. Close hood on grill and open vent slightly. Smoke fish about 1 hour. Baste fish with oil near the end of cooking time. Replace coals, if they begin to die out. Fish is done when surface is golden and flesh flakes easily.

Note:
Trout or mackerel can be prepared in the same manner. Be sure to keep trout moist. Serve this with plenty of beer, cole slaw, and potato salad.

Barbecued Whole Fish

Ingredients:
1 ¾-lb. cleaned fish (red snapper, grouper, or trout) per person
onion slices
fresh herbs, chopped
vegetable oil

Ingredients for Herbed Butter:
½ cup soft butter
2 Tbl. parsley, chopped
¼ tsp. salt
2 Tbl. green onion, minced
½ tsp. fresh tarragon, chopped or 1 tsp. dried tarragon

Directions:
Make Herbed Butter by combining all ingredients. Set aside. Rinse fish well. Pat dry. Stuff cavity with onion slices and any mixture of chopped parsley, oregano, basil, etc., that you have on hand. Oil long-handled grill basket with vegetable oil. Place fish inside. Brush fish with Herbed Butter. Place basket on cooking grill 4-5 inches over medium-hot coals. Cook 10 minutes per inch of fish's thickness, turning once during cooking. Brush with Herbed Butter frequently, to keep fish moist. Fish is done when the flesh is opaque and flakes easily with a fork.

Note:
The choice of fish and herbs on hand makes this recipe always uniquely different.

Italian Baked Oysters

Ingredients for 8 servings:
20 oysters, preferably freshly shucked
2 shallots, minced
1 Tbl. butter
1 Tbl. olive oil
3 tomatoes, peeled, seeded, and chopped
½ cup white wine
2 cups soft bread crumbs
½ cup Parmesan cheese, grated
1 tsp. paprika
⅓ cup butter, melted
1 tsp. dried basil

Directions:
Shuck oysters and set aside, or drain oysters in purchased pint containers. Set aside. In medium saucepan, sauté shallots in butter and olive oil until soft, about 3 minutes. Add tomatoes and wine. Heat over low heat, until mixture becomes a paste, about 30 minutes. In separate bowl, combine bread crumbs, Parmesan cheese, paprika, butter, and basil. In 13-by-9-inch, glass baking dish, layer oysters with tomato paste. Top with bread crumb mixture. Bake at 400° 12 minutes.

Note:
This dish is *so* worth the effort. Excellent as an appetizer or as an entree.

Scalloped Oysters

Ingredients for 12 servings:
2 cups coarse, dry bread crumbs
2 cups oyster crackers, coarsely crushed
2 cups butter, melted
2 pints shucked oysters, drained and liquor reserved
liquor reserved from oysters
1 cup heavy cream
2 Tbl. dry sherry
1 Tbl. Worcestershire sauce
¼ tsp. black pepper, freshly ground
1 tsp. salt
⅛ tsp. cayenne pepper

Directions:
Preheat oven to 375°. Combine bread crumbs, cracker crumbs, and butter. Set aside. Butter 4-oz. ramekins or an 11-by-13-inch glass baking dish. Cover bottom of dish with half of crumb mixture. Add layer of oysters. Top oysters with remaining crumbs. Combine 1 cup reserved oyster liquor, and remaining ingredients in bowl. Pour over crumbs. Bake about 20-30 minutes, or until bubbly around edges.

Note:
From Anne Thornberry of Savannah, who said you can assemble this dish 1 hour in advance.

Top: Pan-Fried Trout with Pecan Butter (page 81)   Bottom: Angel Biscuits (page 17)

Top: Fried Catfish (page 74)　　　　　　　　　Bottom: Welsh Rabbit (page 62)

Bacon Baked Oysters

Ingredients for 4 to 6 servings:
24 fresh oysters, shucked, half of shell
  reserved
6 slices bacon, cut into 1-inch pieces
½ cup mayonnaise
1 cup buttery cracker crumbs, crushed
2 Tbl. fresh chives, minced
1 tsp. hot pepper sauce
½ tsp. Dijon-style mustard
1 tsp. lemon juice
coarse salt
¼ cup Parmesan cheese, grated

Directions:
Shuck oysters. Set aside. In frying pan, cook
bacon until limp; set aside. In small bowl,
combine remaining ingredients, except
coarse salt and Parmesan cheese. Mix well.
Place ½ inch coarse salt in baking dish.
Arrange oysters on salt until they sit firmly.
Top each oyster with crumb mixture. Sprinkle with Parmesan cheese. Place 1 piece of
bacon on top. Bake at 400° 8-10 minutes, or
until oysters are hot and tender.

Note:
    From my friend and talented seafood
cook Vicki Murphy of Atlanta.

Salmon with Lemon Butter

Ingredients for 8 servings:
¼ cup butter, melted
2 Tbl. lemon juice
2 Tbl. fresh parsley, chopped
¼ tsp. dried dill weed
¼ tsp. dried rosemary, crushed
¼ tsp. dried marjoram, crushed
¼ tsp. salt
⅛ tsp. ground black pepper
8 fresh salmon steaks, cut ¾-1 inch thick

Directions:
Combine all ingredients, except salmon.
Prepare charcoal. Baste salmon steaks with
mixture on both sides. Grill over medium-
hot coals about 5 minutes on each side.
When salmon flakes, it is done. Baste during
grilling.

Note:
    You also can broil this salmon. Line
broiler pan with foil. Place salmon fillets on
well-greased rack. Baste with butter mixture. Broil 4 inches from heat, 10 minutes
per inch thickness. *Do not* turn.

Fried Catfish

Ingredients for 6 servings:
6 ¾-1 lb. pan-dressed, farm-raised catfish
1 cup buttermilk
1 Tbl. salt
1 Tbl. black pepper
½ cup self-rising cornmeal
½ cup self-rising flour
1½-2 quarts peanut oil

Directions:
Wash fish. Drain. Make ⅛-inch slit down the thick part of each side of fish. Place fish in glass bowl. Pour buttermilk over. Add salt and pepper. Cover. Chill 4-6 hours, or overnight. Remove fish from buttermilk. Drain well. Combine cornmeal and flour in shallow pan. Roll fish in mixture, coating all sides. Heat oil to 370° in deep fat fryer or deep skillet. Place fish in oil, a few at a time, and fry until they are golden brown and no longer leak water when squeezed with tongs. Drain on absorbent brown paper. Transfer fish to wire rack and place in warm oven, to stay crisp.

Note:
This tastes best when served with cole slaw and hush puppies.

Catfish Amandine

Ingredients for 6 servings:
2 lbs. farm-raised catfish fillets
½ cup flour
1 tsp. seasoned salt
1 tsp. paprika
4 Tbl. butter, melted
½ cup almonds, sliced
2 Tbl. lemon juice
1 Tbl. parsley, chopped
4 drops Tabasco sauce

Directions:
Cut fish into serving-sized portions. Combine flour, seasoned salt, and paprika. Dredge fish in flour mixture. Place, skin side down, in well-greased 10-by-13-inch broiler pan. Drizzle 2 Tbl. of the butter over fish.

Broil about 4 inches from heat 8-10 minutes, or until fish flakes with fork. While fish is broiling, place remaining 2 Tbl. butter in saucepan. Add almonds. Cook over medium heat, stirring until golden brown. Remove from heat. Add lemon juice, parsley, and Tabasco sauce. Pour sauce over fish.

Note:
Catfish fillets work well in any recipes calling for fish with firm, white flesh.

Seafood Sausage

Ingredients for 10 4-oz. sausages:
½ lb. large shrimp, shelled and deveined
½ lb. fresh salmon, bones and skin
  removed
3 egg whites
crushed ice
¼ cup milk
½ lb. bay scallops *or* sea scallops,
  washed and diced
½ lb. fresh salmon, bones and skin
  removed, diced
¼ cup shallots, minced
1 Tbl. butter
3-4 cups fresh spinach, chopped
1 bunch watercress, chopped
dash salt *or* salt substitute
dash white pepper
dash nutmeg
1 Tbl. fresh chives, diced
1 Tbl. fresh tarragon, diced
1 Tbl. fresh parsley, diced
1 Tbl. fresh basil, diced
butter
fish stock *or* chicken broth, to poach
fresh tomatoes, diced, as garnish
  (optional)
cucumbers, cleaned, peeled, seeded, and
  sliced into julienne strips, as garnish
  (optional)
fresh herbs, chopped, as garnish
  (optional)

Directions:
In food processor, purée shrimp and ½ lb. undiced salmon with egg whites 3 minutes. Place purée in bowl over crushed ice. Add milk, scallops, and ½ lb. diced salmon. Blend well. Cook shallots in 1 Tbl. butter over low heat, until transparent. Add spinach and watercress. Toss lightly for 1 minute. Season with salt, pepper, and nutmeg. Chill. Add cooled spinach mixture and fresh herbs to fish mixture. Blend well. Cut aluminum foil into 10 4-inch-by-5-inch squares. Rub lightly with butter. Place about ½ cup of mixture in each foil square. Roll into sausage shape. Seal ends well. Bring fish stock to boil in large saucepan. Cover sausage with stock and simmer for 8 minutes. Garnish sausages with tomatoes, cucumbers, or more fresh herbs.

Note:
    If fresh herbs are not available, used dried herbs. Instead of 1 Tbl. each, use 1 tsp.
    Each sausage is about 137 calories.
    This recipe is from the Spa at Sonoma Mission Inn, 40 miles north of San Francisco.

Acadian Peppered Shrimp

Ingredients for 4 servings:
4 lbs. medium shrimp in shells
1 lb. butter
¼ cup lemon juice
2 tsp. dried basil
1½ tsp. cayenne pepper
1 tsp. dried oregano
5 cloves garlic, minced
1 bay leaf, minced
½ cup black pepper, finely ground
dash nutmeg

Directions:
Rinse shrimp and drain well. Melt butter in 14-inch, deep-sided skillet over low heat. When melted, add remaining ingredients. Bring heat to medium. Cook, stirring, 15 minutes, or until butter has browned to rich hazelnut color. Add shrimp. Cook, stirring, about 10 minutes, or until shrimp has turned rich, coral color.

Note:
    From Terry Thompson, accomplished New Orleans cooking instructor, who prepared this for a class at Rich's Cooking School. It is very hot, messy, and fun to eat.

Rock Shrimp Manquechou

Ingredients for 4 to 6 servings:
4 slices bacon, chopped
1 large onion, chopped
3 cloves garlic, minced
½ cup green pepper, chopped
2 cups fresh or frozen corn kernels
2½ cups tomatoes, chopped, peeled, and
    drained, liquid reserved
liquid reserved from tomatoes
reserved oyster liquor and water to make
    1 cup
¼ tsp. cayenne pepper
1½ tsp. salt
½ lb. rock shrimp, peeled and deveined
½ pint oysters, drained, reserving liquor

Directions:
In heavy, 4-quart casserole, cook bacon until limp. Add onion, garlic, and green pepper. Cook about 3 minutes, or until onion is translucent, but not browned. Stir in corn and tomatoes. Add tomato liquid, reserved oyster liquor, cayenne pepper, and salt. Simmer mixture 10 minutes, or until corn is tender. Add rock shrimp and oysters. Cook 2 minutes, or until oysters begin to curl. Serve with hot bread and slaw.

Note:
    Rock shrimp are a less expensive alternative to regular shrimp.

Sesame Shrimp and Asparagus

Ingredients for 6 servings:
¼ cup vegetable oil
1 lb. fresh asparagus, cut on the diagonal into 2-inch pieces
1 medium onion, sliced
1½ lbs. large shrimp, peeled and deveined
4-5 tsp. soy sauce
2 Tbl. sesame seeds, toasted
salt, to taste (optional)
black pepper to taste (optional)

Directions:
Heat oil in large skillet or wok over medium-high heat. Stir-fry asparagus, onion, and shrimp, until shrimp are pink and vegetables are crisp-tender, about 5 minutes. Remove from heat. Stir in soy sauce and sesame seeds. Season with salt and pepper. Serve over rice, or serve hot with toothpicks as an hors d'oeuvre.

Note:
Toast sesame seeds for 5 minutes at 350°.

Shrimp Feta

Ingredients for 6 servings:
2 cups onion, chopped
2 cloves garlic, minced
2 Tbl. butter
2 Tbl. olive oil
4 cups fresh tomatoes, peeled, seeded, and chopped
1 tsp. dried dill weed *or* 1 Tbl. fresh dill weed, minced
1 tsp. dried basil *or* 1 Tbl. fresh basil, minced
1 tsp. dry mustard
1 tsp. sugar
½ cup parsley, chopped
1 tsp. salt
½ tsp. black pepper
2 lbs. large shrimp, peeled and deveined
½ cup white wine
½ lb. feta cheese, crumbled

Directions:
In large skillet with cover, sauté onion and garlic in butter and olive oil, until golden. Stir in tomatoes, dill, basil, mustard, sugar, parsley, salt, and pepper. Simmer 5 minutes. Add shrimp and wine. Continue simmering, stirring, 3 minutes or until shrimp has cooked through. Don't overcook. Turn off heat. Sprinkle cheese over skillet. Cover with lid. Let sit 2 minutes, or until cheese has slightly melted. Serve from skillet with crusty French bread and green salad.

Baked Grouper with Fresh Tomato Sauce

Ingredients for 8 servings:
2 Tbl. vegetable oil
8 5-6-oz. fillets — grouper, scrod *or* red
   snapper
salt, to taste
white pepper, to taste
butter, melted (optional)
½ cup dry bread crumbs
2 Tbl. butter

Ingredients for Fresh Tomato Sauce:
½ cup onion, chopped
2 Tbl. butter
6 tomatoes, chopped
2 cloves garlic
2 Tbl. parsley, chopped
½ tsp. salt
½ tsp. black pepper
½ tsp. dried basil

Directions:
Preheat oven to 350°. Take glass baking dish large enough to hold fish. Cover bottom with vegetable oil. Sprinkle fillets on both sides with salt and pepper. Lay in dish in 1 layer. If desired, pour on a little melted butter, to keep fish moist. Bake 15 minutes. While fish is baking, sauté bread crumbs in 2 Tbl. butter, until golden. Sprinkle bread crumb mixture over dish. Bake 10 minutes. Remove. Serve with sauce.

To make sauce, sauté ½ cup onion in 2 Tbl. butter in medium skillet. Stir in remaining sauce ingredients. Transfer mixture to bowl of food processor. Purée. Return to skillet and heat briefly, just to warm sauce. Serve over fish.

Crab Cakes

Ingredients for 6 to 8 Crab Cakes:
1 egg, well beaten
2 Tbl. mayonnaise
1 Tbl. Dijon-style mustard
1 Tbl. butter, melted
1 tsp. fresh parsley, chopped
½ tsp. dry mustard
½ tsp. seafood seasoning (Old Bay)
salt, to taste
pepper, to taste
¼ cup dry bread crumbs
1 lb. lump crab meat, all shell removed
½ cup dry bread crumbs
oil, to fry

Directions:
Mix together all ingredients except crab meat and ½ cup bread crumbs. Gently fold in crab meat, careful not to break lumps. Shape into 6-8 cakes. Roll in remainder of bread crumbs to coat. Fry in deep fat heated to 375° until golden brown, about 3-4 minutes.

Note:
Rich, rich, but oh so good. Dunk in hot mustard, for a special treat.

Steamed Blue Crabs

Ingredients for 6 servings as an appetizer or 3 servings as a meal:
3 cups water
3 cups cider vinegar
3 dozen live blue crabs
½ cup seafood seasoning (Old Bay is good)
¼ cup salt

Directions:
In bottom of large pot with rack and tightly-fitting lid, place water, vinegar, and crabs. Sprinkle seafood seasoning and salt over layers of live crabs, as they are dropped in pot. Cover pot. Bring to boil. Reduce heat. Simmer about 20-30 minutes, or until crabs turn red in color.

Note:
The bigger the crab, the better; there's less work for more crab meat.

Grouper in White Wine

Ingredients for 6 servings:
1 4-5-lb. grouper, gutted and scaled
salt
pepper
garlic powder
1 tsp. dried thyme
3 Tbl. butter
1 Tbl. butter
1 bay leaf
2 Tbl. butter
1 bunch green onions, chopped
8 oz. mushrooms, sliced
1 cup white wine
dash paprika
½ cup bread crumbs

Directions:
Preheat oven to 350°. Depending on size of the open glass or earthenware casserole dish you have, you may need to cut the head and tail from fish. Sprinkle salt and pepper in cavity. Dust lightly with garlic powder and thyme. Melt 3 Tbl. butter in bottom of dish by placing it in oven for few minutes. Place 1 Tbl. butter and bay leaf in fish cavity. Place fish in baking dish. Dot remaining 2 Tbl. butter on outside. Toss green onions and mushrooms over fish. Pour wine over all. Sprinkle with paprika and bread crumbs. Cook uncovered, 1 hour to 1 hour, 15 minutes.

Grilled Tuna Steaks

Ingredients for 2 generous servings or 3
  to 4 adequate servings:
¼ cup olive oil
1 Tbl. red wine vinegar
½ tsp. kosher salt
⅛ tsp. black pepper, freshly ground
2 cloves garlic, crushed
1½ lbs. fresh tuna steaks 1¼-inch thick
  (*or* halibut steaks *or* swordfish steaks)

Directions:
Combine oil, vinegar, salt, pepper, and garlic in glass bowl large enough to hold steaks. Add steaks to marinade. Let marinate several hours or overnight, refrigerated.
    To grill, let charcoal burn to gray ash. Rub grill with oil, to prevent sticking. Place steaks on grill. Cook 5-10 minutes per side, or until fish is just opaque. Serve immediately, topped with soft butter and sprinkled with chopped chives. Serve with roasted peppers, charred alongside the fish on grill, peeled and doused with olive oil, lemon juice, and crushed garlic. Perhaps top the peppers with grated Parmesan cheese.

Note:
From Elaine Reader.

Pan-Fried Trout with Pecan Butter

Ingredients for 4 servings:
4 trout fillets
flour, for dredging
butter, for frying
½ cup butter
⅓ cup pecans, chopped
2 tsp. chives, minced
1 tsp. lemon juice

Directions:
Lightly flour fillets. Pan fry in small amount of butter over medium heat for 2 minutes on first side and 1 minute on other. Remove fish from pan (keep warm). In separate saucepan, melt ½ cup butter. Add remaining ingredients. Stir over low heat, until well combined. Ladle pecan butter over fillets. Serve.

Note:
The flavor of this dish is so delicate that you might serve it as a first course to a fine meal.

Fried Rainbow Trout

Ingredients for 6 servings:
6 whole rainbow trout, cleaned
salt, to taste
black pepper, to taste
white cornmeal
vegetable oil
2 Tbl. bacon drippings
Cucumber Sauce (see page 194)

Directions:
Season trout with salt and pepper. Roll in cornmeal, which can be seasoned with salt and pepper if you like. Pour oil into heavy, cast-iron skillet until it comes ½ inch up the sides. Add bacon drippings. Heat oil, until it reaches 370° or until a drop of water sizzles when it hits the pan. Place trout in grease. Fry until golden brown — about 7 minutes to a side. Serve hot with Cucumber Sauce.

Note:
While most people wouldn't dare fry rainbow trout, the prize of north Georgia mountain streams, you should try it at least once.

Grilled Shark Steaks

Ingredients for 4 servings:
4 shark steaks, 1-inch thick
water
juice of 8 limes
2 Tbl. fresh parsley, minced
2 Tbl. fresh chives, minced
salt, to taste
black pepper, freshly ground, to taste
butter, melted
paprika

Directions:
Parboil steaks 5 minutes in minimum of water. Drain. When cool enough to handle, peel off skin. Place steaks in glass dish large enough to hold them in one layer. Squeeze lime juice over all. Marinate steaks 6-8 hours, covered, in the refrigerator. When ready to grill, sprinkle parsley, chives, salt, and pepper generously over steaks. Cook over low coals on greased grill about 5 minutes per side, 10 minutes cooking time in all. When steaks are done, brush both sides with melted butter. Sprinkle with paprika.

Note:
     From Kim Hoagland, Lanier Sailing Academy.

Poultry

Perfectly Fried Chicken

Like making biscuits and pie crusts, frying chicken is an art that cooks master with time. There are few cases of beginner's luck, but there are certain tips which can help your chicken turn out golden and crispy on the outside, juicy and tender on the inside:

• Freshness is important. Frozen chicken will not do.

• For maximum flavor, fry chicken in lard. However, a corn, soybean, or peanut oil will work quite well, because they can reach the high temperatures needed for frying crisp chicken without smoking or discoloring. For best results, do not recycle oil after frying.

• A 2-inch depth of oil in the skillet produces the crispiest chicken. Add a tablespoon of bacon grease to vegetable oil for well-flavored chicken.

• When frying any food, fry hot enough so that the skin seals in juices and the meat steams itself to doneness. That way, no fat seeps into the chicken. Most cooks feel that 350° is hot enough.

• To flavor chicken, some cooks soak it in buttermilk before frying. The buttermilk actually tenderizes the bird and imparts some flavor, too. I like to soak chicken pieces in ice water 30 minutes to 1 hour to draw out the blood. Then rinse and dredge it in flour seasoned with salt and pepper. That's it.

• Whether to fry chicken in an open or closed skillet is a hot debate. I prefer the closed pan, because it traps heat in the pan and steams chicken done, and it also traps spatters of grease that might land on your kitchen walls.

• Turn chicken only once while frying, and turn it with a spoon, not a fork. The tines of a fork pierce chicken, allowing juices out and grease in.

• Large pieces of chicken need to cook at least 25 minutes and smaller pieces at least 20 minutes.

• One last note: True Southern-fried chicken should not be smothered with gravy. After going to the trouble, why spoil your crisp crust?

Bacon-Wrapped Chicken

Ingredients for 4 servings:
4 boned, skinned chicken breasts
3 oz. cream cheese
4 tsp. green onion, minced
1 tsp. dried tarragon
1 tsp. black pepper
8 slices bacon

Directions:
Split breasts horizontally, so they open flat, like a book. In center of each, place ¼ cheese, green onion, tarragon, and black pepper. Roll up tightly. Wrap each roll with 2 slices bacon and secure with wooden picks. Place over medium coals of charcoal grill or under broiler. Cook 10 minutes on one side, turn and cook 10 minues on other, or until bacon is crisp.

Note:
   May be served as an entree or sliced and served as hors d'oeuvres.

Lemon-Rosemary Chicken

Ingredients for 6 servings:
1 tsp. dried rosemary, crushed
2 cloves garlic, minced
6 boned chicken breast halves
salt, to taste
black pepper, to taste
2 lemons
4 Tbl. butter

Directions:
Preheat oven to 350°. Mix rosemary and garlic. Flatten chicken breasts with palm of hand or back of a knife. Arrange them on large sheet of foil. Season with salt and pepper. Sprinkle rosemary-garlic mixture over chicken. Slice lemons. Put 2-3 slices on each breast. Dot with butter. Seal foil into packet. Place on baking sheet. Bake 30 minutes.

Note:
   A simple dish to prepare in the morning, refrigerate, and heat just before dinner. Serve with rice and steamed broccoli or asparagus.

Parmesan Chicken Rolls

Ingredients for 4 to 6 servings:
4 whole chicken breasts, halved, boned, and skinned
½ cup butter
1½ cups dry bread crumbs
1 cup Parmesan cheese, grated
1 clove garlic, minced

Directions:
Preheat oven to 325°. Rinse chicken breasts. Drain well. Melt butter in small saucepan. Combine bread crumbs, Parmesan cheese, and garlic in small bowl. Dip chicken breasts, 1 at time, in butter. Then dredge on all sides in crumb mixture. Beginning at narrow end of chicken, roll up into fat cigar shapes. Place, seam side down, in 9-by-13-inch baking dish. Drizzle remaining butter over top. Bake about 1½ hours, or until chicken is well browned, crisp, and fork can be inserted in chicken with ease. Serve with rice and gravy made from drippings from pan, if desired.

Note:
    The first time I tasted this dish, dreamed up by my mother, it was served cold. It's delicious both ways.

Lemon Roasted Chicken

Ingredients for 6 to 8 servings:
8 chicken quarters
1 cup Dijon-style mustard
½ cup apricot jam
¼ cup lemon juice

Directions:
Preheat oven to 375°. Pat chicken dry with paper towels. Place in roasting pan in oven. Roast 40 minutes, or until about ¾ done. Remove from oven. Combine mustard, jam, and lemon juice in small bowl. Blend well. Brush mustard mixture on both sides of chicken. Bake, skin side up, about 10-15 minutes more, or until golden brown. Serve hot or cold. Remaining sauce can be used for dipping.

Note:
    From Kay Goldstein, Proof of the Pudding, Atlanta, Georgia.

Country Captain Chicken

Ingredients for 4 servings:
8 chicken thighs, washed and patted dry
salt, to taste
black pepper, to taste
2 Tbl. butter
1 medium onion, chopped
½ cup green pepper, seeded and thinly
  sliced
2 cloves garlic, minced
¼ cup celery, chopped
1 24-oz. can Italian plum tomatoes,
  drained and crushed
¾ tsp. salt
¼ tsp. black pepper
½ tsp. dried thyme
1 Tbl. curry powder
¼ cup currants
¼ cup almonds, toasted and slivered

Directions:
Salt and pepper chicken. In large skillet, melt butter. Brown chicken on both sides. Remove to platter to stay warm. Pour off all but 2 Tbl. drippings. In drippings, sauté onion, pepper, garlic, and celery, until onion is opaque. Add tomatoes. Reduce heat. Simmer 15 minutes. Add salt, pepper, thyme, and curry powder to skillet. Simmer 5 minutes. Return chicken to skillet. Simmer 20 minutes, or until chicken is tender. If liquid begins to evaporate too quickly, cover skillet. Just before serving, add currants and almonds to skillet. Mix well. Serve atop fluffy rice and with mango chutney to the side.

Note:
    From Anne Thornberry, Savannah, Georgia.

Chicken Spinach Lasagna

Ingredients for 8 servings:
8 chicken breast halves
water
6 Tbl. butter
8 Tbl. flour
1½ cups buttermilk
1½ cups half-and-half
salt, to taste
black pepper, to taste
3 10-oz. packages frozen chopped
   spinach, thawed and drained
4 oz. cream cheese, softened
6 oz. ricotta
8 ounces jarlsberg cheese, shredded
¼ cup dry white wine
salt, to taste
pepper, to taste
nutmeg, to taste
½ lb. lasagna noodles
about ½ cup Parmesan cheese, grated

Directions:
Preheat oven to 350°. Place chicken breasts in small stock pot with water to cover. Bring to boil. Reduce heat. Simmer about 20 minutes, or until chicken is cooked through.

In medium saucepan, melt butter. Whisk in flour until smooth and a paste has formed. Stir in buttermilk, half-and-half, salt, and pepper. Stir briefly until mixture is smooth and has thickened. Set aside.

Remove skin and bones from chicken. Break into small pieces. In large mixing bowl, combine chicken, spinach, cream cheese, ricotta, jarlsberg and about ¼ cup wine to moisten. Add about ¼ to ½ cup sauce to mixture. Combine. Add salt, pepper, and nutmeg. Pour ¼ cup sauce into 9-by-11-inch, glass baking dish. Spread evenly over bottom. Add layer of uncooked lasagna noodles. Douse liberally with wine. Add layer of chicken-spinach filling and another layer of sauce. Place another layer of noodles on sauce. Douse with wine. Top with more filling and end with layer of sauce. Sprinkle with Parmesan cheese, to cover top. Bake about 1 hour.

Note:
   This rich casserole needs only sliced, fresh tomatoes as an accompaniment.

Chicken Pot Pie

Ingredients for 4 to 6 servings:
¼ cup butter
¼ cup flour
2 cups milk
½ tsp. salt
black pepper, to taste
2 cups chicken, cooked and diced
1 10-oz. package frozen peas, thawed and drained

Ingredients for Pastry:
½ cup butter, room temperature
3 oz. cream cheese, room temperature
1 cup flour

Directions:
Preheat oven to 450°. Make pastry: Blend together butter and cream cheese. With two sharp knives, work and cut in flour, until blended. Chill, tightly wrapped, until firm enough to handle.

Melt butter in 2-quart saucepan. Whisk in flour. When smooth, add milk, salt, and pepper. Cook over low heat, whisking, until mixture thickens. Take sauce off heat. Add chicken and peas. Stir to combine.

On floured board, roll out pastry to 7-by-11-inch rectangle. Turn chicken mixture into 1½-quart rectangular baking dish. Place pastry over dish, sealing edges to sides. Cut 4 1-inch vents across center of pastry. Cut another slanted vent at each corner. Bake 20-25 minutes, or until pastry is golden brown and chicken hot.

Parmesan Chicken

Ingredients for 8 servings:
½ cup olive oil
1 clove garlic, minced
2 cups dry bread crumbs
¾ cup Parmesan cheese, grated
1 tsp. salt
½ tsp. black pepper
8 chicken breast halves

Directions:
Preheat oven to 350°. Heat olive oil in small saucepan. Add garlic. Remove pan from heat. In separate bowl, combine bread crumbs, Parmesan cheese, salt, and pepper. Brush chicken with olive oil mixture. Dredge with bread crumb mixture. Place in 10-by-13-inch, ungreased baking pan. Bake, uncovered, 1 hour, or until fork can be inserted in chicken with ease, and crust is crisp and golden.

Fried Chicken (page 83)

The Best Turkey Dressing (page 31)

Stuffed Chicken Breasts with Dill Butter Sauce

Ingredients for 4 servings:
4 6-oz. chicken breasts, skinned and
  boned
8 oz. herb-garlic cheese
3 eggs
¼ cup milk
flour, as needed
2 cups dry bread crumbs
vegetable oil, for frying

Ingredients for Dill Butter Sauce:
2 Tbl. shallots, minced
½ cup dry white wine
1½ Tbl. fresh lemon juice
¾ cup heavy cream
½ tsp. hot pepper sauce
1 tsp. salt
1 Tbl. dill weed
1 cup unsalted butter, cut into pieces

Directions:
Make Dill Butter Sauce: Combine shallots, wine, and lemon juice in saucepan. Simmer over moderate heat, until liquid has reduced to 2 Tbl.

Add cream. Reduce again, until liquid is ½ cup. Stir in pepper sauce, salt, and dill weed. Set aside.

Flatten chicken breasts between layers of wax paper, until ¼ inch thick. Spread quarter of herb-garlic cheese on each. Fold breasts in half. Tuck under ends. Chill 1 hour.

Preheat oven to 400°. Beat eggs. Add milk. Dredge chicken in flour and dip in egg wash. Then coat with bread crumbs. Heat oil in large sauté pan. Add chicken breasts, 1 at a time. Brown on both sides. Remove from pan. Place on cookie sheet. Bake 8-10 minutes.

Just before serving chicken, heat sauce. Whip in pieces of butter slowly. Stir constantly. *Do not* allow sauce to boil. When butter is incorporated, serve at once.

Note:
This Dill Butter Sauce recipe makes about 1 cup. It is also good with steamed vegetables and poached fish.

From Houlihan's Restaurant in Lenox Square, Atlanta, Georgia.

Swiss Smothered Chicken

Ingredients for 10 servings:
5 whole chicken breasts, split, skinned, and boned
salt
2 eggs, beaten
1 cup dry bread crumbs
¼ cup vegetable oil
3 Tbl. butter
¼ cup flour
½ tsp. salt
⅛ tsp. black pepper, freshly ground
2½ cups milk
½ cup dry white wine
1 cup Swiss cheese, shredded
1 tomato, cut into wedges
1 small avocado, peeled, seeded, and sliced

Directions:
Place chicken breasts between 2 pieces of wax paper. Pound to ¼-inch thickness. Sprinkle with salt. Dip into egg, then into bread crumbs. Brown chicken in oil, 2 minutes per side. Remove chicken from pan. Set aside. In separate pan, melt butter. Blend in flour, salt, and pepper. Gradually add milk, stirring. Cook until thick. Remove from heat. Stir in wine. Pour half of sauce into bottom of 2-by-9-by-13-inch baking dish. Arrange cutlets on sauce. Top with remaining sauce. Cover. Chill several hours. Preheat oven to 350°. Bake, covered, until heated through, about 50 minutes. Sprinkle with cheese. Top with tomato wedges and avocado slices. Bake 2 minutes.

Note:
For a make-ahead buffet dish, you can't beat this one. Assemble early in the day and stick in the refrigerator until serving time. You can even freeze it, thaw until it reaches room temperature, add cheese, and proceed.

Cuban Chicken

Ingredients for 8 servings:
1 3½-lb. chicken, cut into pieces
3 Tbl. olive oil
3 cloves garlic, peeled and mashed
2 medium onions, chopped
1 green bell pepper, seeded and chopped
1 16-oz. can tomatoes, undrained
2 large bay leaves
1 pinch saffron
salt, to taste
black pepper, freshly ground, to taste
4 cups water
2 cups raw rice
1 cup dry sherry *or* dry red wine
1 3-4-oz. jar pimientos, chopped and
   drained
1 6-8-oz. can small green peas, drained
1 14-oz. can artichoke hearts, drained

Directions:
Brown chicken in skillet in olive oil, until brown and crispy on both sides. Add garlic, onion, and pepper to skillet. Sauté 3-4 minutes; stir to prevent burning. Add tomatoes, bay leaves, saffron, salt, and pepper. Cover. Simmer 10 minutes.

Cover mixture with water. Bring to boil. Reduce heat. Cover. Simmer until chicken is tender — about 30-40 minutes. Add rice. Continue cooking, covered, until water in pan is absorbed, and rice is done. Add sherry or wine. Cover. Simmer 5 minutes.

Before serving, top skillet mixture with pimientos, peas, and artichokes. Cover. Allow to steam for few minutes, or until all is heated through.

Note:
From Sarita Gonzalez, owner of Sarita's Cuban Restaurant in Atlanta. This recipe is fool-proof.

Chicken Dijon

Ingredients for 6 servings:
4 Tbl. flour
1 tsp. salt
¼ tsp. black pepper, freshly ground
4 1-lb. chicken breasts, halved, boned,
  and skinned
2 Tbl. butter
2 Tbl. vegetable oil
2 Tbl. butter
2 Tbl. flour
3 Tbl. Dijon-style mustard
1 cup heavy cream
¾ cup dry white wine
1 tsp. salt
¼ tsp. dried tarragon

Directions:
Preheat oven to 325°. Mix 4 Tbl. flour, salt,
and pepper in small bowl. Dredge chicken
breasts on all sides with mixture. In medium
skillet, heat 2 Tbl. butter and oil. Sauté
chicken breasts on both sides, until golden
and almost cooked through, about 8-10
minutes per side. Remove chicken to baking
pan. Bake about 15 minutes.
   Meanwhile, melt 2 Tbl. butter in saucepan. Whisk in 2 Tbl. flour. Cook until all
flour is incorporated. Whisk in mustard.
Whisk in remaining ingredients. Cook,
whisking constantly, until mixture is thick.
Remove chicken from oven. Pour sauce over
chicken while hot. Serve with rice and fresh
fruit.

Note:
   The sauce of this dish is especially good.
To add color, garnish top with minced
parsley.

Turkey Mornay

Ingredients for 4 to 6 servings:
1 bunch fresh broccoli
8-10 slices cooked turkey breast
4 Tbl. butter
3 Tbl. flour
1 cup chicken broth
1 cup half-and-half
1 egg yolk
3 Tbl. heavy cream
2 tsp. Worcestershire sauce
salt, to taste
black pepper, freshly ground, to taste
¼ cup dry sherry
¼ cup Parmesan cheese, freshly grated
¼ cup Gruyere *or* Swiss cheese, shredded
nutmeg, freshly grated, to taste
cayenne pepper, to taste
¼ cup Parmesan cheese, grated

Directions:
Steam broccoli or cook in boiling water until crisp-tender. Drain. Slice lengthwise. Arrange in bottom of shallow baking dish. Place turkey slices over it.

Preheat oven to 400°. Melt butter in heavy saucepan. Add flour. Stir to form smooth roux or paste. Cook 2 minutes, stirring. Remove saucepan from heat. Pour in broth and half-and-half, stirring constantly. Return saucepan to low heat. Cook, stirring, until thick and bubbly. Beat egg yolk and cream together. Spoon 3 Tbl. hot sauce into egg-cream mixture. Stir well.

Pour back into remaining sauce. Add Worcestershire sauce, salt, pepper, sherry, ¼ cup of the Parmesan cheese, Swiss or Gruyere cheese, nutmeg, and cayenne pepper. Cook over low heat, until cheese is melted, stirring. Pour sauce over turkey, covering well. Sprinkle top with ¼ cup Parmesan cheese. Bake 20 minutes, or until top is lightly browned and bubbly.

Note:
You can substitute sliced chicken breasts for turkey, and frozen broccoli or steamed fresh asparagus (1½ lbs.) for fresh broccoli.

Smoked Turkey

Ingredients for 12 servings:
charcoal
hickory chips, soaked in water
1 12-lb. fresh turkey
salt
butter, melted

Directions:
Light charcoal in covered barbecue grill or meat smoker. After about 50-60 minutes, add hickory chips to coals, to create smoke.

Remove giblets from the turkey. Wash turkey. Dry well. Sprinkle salt inside cavity and over outside of bird. Brush well with melted butter. Oil grill well. Place turkey on grill positioned at least 1 foot from the coals. Baste periodically with melted butter. Cook, covered, about 4-5 hours, or until a meat thermometer inserted into thigh meat registers 185°. You will need to replenish the fire with charcoal and soaked hickory chips during cooking. If the bird begins to darken too early, tent it with foil. Should you desire to save the drippings for gravy, simply cook turkey in disposable aluminum pan the first 1½ hours. Reserve drippings, and place bird on grill to finish cooking.

Roast Turkey Breast

Ingredients for 12 to 15 servings:
1 5-7 lb. turkey breast
butter, melted
salt, to taste
black pepper, freshly ground, to taste
½ cup white wine

Directions:
Preheat oven to 325°. Wash turkey breast. Pat dry. Brush well with melted butter on all sides. Sprinkle liberally with salt and pepper. Arrange rack in roasting pan. Roast 20 minutes per lb. or until the internal temperature of the turkey reaches 160°-165° degrees. During roasting process, add wine to drippings. Baste bird with mixture every 20 minutes. Let cool slightly, before slicing.

Note:
For added flavor, insert whole onion and sprigs of fresh parsley or tarragon in cavity, before roasting.

Turkey Marsala

Ingredients for 8 to 10 servings:
1 3-3½ lb. turkey breast, sliced ¼-inch
  thick
¾ cup flour
½ tsp. salt
½ tsp. pepper
½ tsp. garlic powder
2 Tbl. olive oil
2 Tbl. butter
1 cup parsley, chopped
1 tsp. dried basil *or* 1 Tbl. fresh basil,
  minced
3 cloves garlic, minced
1 lb. fresh mushrooms, sliced
2½ cups chicken broth
¾ cup Marsala

Directions:
Pound turkey to ⅛-inch thickness. Dredge
in flour seasoned with salt, pepper, and
garlic powder. Shake off excess flour. Place 1
Tbl. oil and 1 Tbl. butter in skillet. Heat.
Sauté turkey on both sides just until the pink
color is gone, adding more butter and oil, as
necessary. Remove pieces to platter to keep
warm. Use as little oil as possible during this
process. Add parsley, basil, and garlic to
pan. Sauté 1 minute, stirring. Add mushrooms to pan. Cover. Steam 5-7 minutes, or
until liquid is produced. Add broth and wine
to skillet, stirring and scraping up browned
bits on bottom. Heat until bubbly. Simmer 5
minutes. Remove pan from heat. Serve over
sautéed turkey pieces.

Note:
  Turkey parts are an inexpensive alternative to purchasing veal. You can use turkey
breasts in most recipes calling for veal
cutlets.

Smoked Turkey Tettrazini

Ingredients for 4 servings:
3 Tbl. butter
2 Tbl. flour
1½ cups turkey *or* chicken stock
dash Tabasco sauce
salt, to taste
black pepper, freshly ground, to taste
2 Tbl. butter
½ lb. fresh mushrooms, sliced
water
½ lb. linguine
1 Tbl. dry sherry
2 Tbl. heavy cream
¼ cup almonds, sliced and toasted
3 cups smoked turkey, shredded
1 cup Parmesan cheese, grated

Directions:
Preheat oven to 375°. In large saucepan, melt 3 Tbl. butter. Add flour, stirring well. Cook 2 minutes. Add stock, Tabasco sauce, salt, and pepper. Cook, stirring, over low heat until thickened.

In small pan, melt 2 Tbl. butter. Add mushrooms. Sauté, until mushrooms begin to render their juices.

Cook linguine in rapidly boiling water. Cook according to package directions or to *al dente*.

Add sherry, cream, almonds, turkey, and mushrooms to sauce. Continue to simmer until turkey is heated.

Drain linguine. Place in buttered, 2-quart casserole. Pour sauce over all. Sprinkle with Parmesan cheese. Dot with remaining 1 Tbl. butter. Bake 20-30 minutes. Serve hot.

Note:
Of course, unsmoked turkey breast also can be used in this recipe.

Duck with Orange-Raspberry Sauce

Ingredients for 4 servings:
1 4-5 lb. duckling, giblets and neck
  removed
1 tsp. salt
½ tsp. white pepper
2 cups bread cubes, toasted
1 cup celery, chopped
1 cup pitted prunes, chopped
1 cup apples, diced
½ cup onion, chopped
¼ cup packed light brown sugar
2 Tbl. orange juice
3 Tbl. flour
2 cups orange juice
1 cup black raspberry jam

Directions:
Preheat oven to 450°. Remove wing tips
from duck. Rub cavity with salt and pepper.
Fasten neck skin and wings to back with
cotton kitchen twine; set duck aside. Toss
bread cubes, celery, prunes, apples, and
onion together. Stuff mixture lightly into
duck's body cavity. Close with skewers. Tie
legs close to body. Place, breast side down,
on rack in shallow roasting pan. Roast 30
minutes. Reduce heat to 350°. Turn breast
side up and roast 1 hour more, draining off
fat as it accumulates. Meanwhile, mix brown
sugar with 2 Tbl. orange juice. Remove
skewers from duck. Roast 30 minutes
longer, brushing with brown sugar mixture
and basting with pan juices several times,
until skin is brown and crisp, and drumstick
feels soft when pressed. Remove duck to
platter. Keep warm. Drain off from pan all
but 3 Tbl. fat. Place on low heat. Stir in flour,
until smooth. Gradually add 2 cups juice,
scraping up browned bits in pan. Stir in jam,
until blended. Cook sauce, stirring, about 10
minutes, or until thickened. Cut duck into
quarters. Serve with sauce.

Note:
Although wild duck is hunted throughout the South, the domestic variety can be
found easily at supermarkets. It is much
plumper than the wild variety.

Dillard Munford's Quail

Ingredients for 3 to 4 servings:
6 quail, cleaned and dressed
½ cup butter
2 Tbl. Worcestershire sauce
juice of 1 lemon
black pepper, to taste
garlic salt, to taste

Directions:
Wash and drain quail. Set aside. In small saucepan, melt butter. Add Worcestershire sauce, lemon, pepper, and garlic salt. Place lemon halves back in sauce. Set aside. When charcoal coals are hot but almost a gray ash, sop birds with sauce and place on grill, about 6 inches from coals. Cook 8 minutes to a side. Baste twice during cooking. Test one quail. If meat is very light pink, remove from grill. Pour any excess sauce over birds. Serve.

Note:
   Dillard Munford of Majik Market fame loves quail, but his convenience stores don't sell them.

Meats

Pit-Cooking the Pig

Barbecue is the English adaptation of the Spanish *barbacoa,* which describes the outdoor grilling of meat by Indians in Haiti. Barbecue in the South, except for the Southwest, where beef is most popular, is synonymous with pork.

It is the whole hog which is so lovingly prepared by outdoor chefs from the Carolinas south and west. But pit-cooking a pig is no easy task. It requires the physical labor of boosting the pig onto the grill and turning the massive 100-pound-plus animal during the process. It requires culinary aptitude — being able to prepare not only 1 gallon of barbecue sauce well, but 30 gallons to swab the meat. And it requires patience to wait out the long, often laborious cooking process.

The returns, however, are well worth the wait. Sweet, slow-cooked pork barbecue tastes all the better when you have assisted in the effort.

At the 1983 Memphis in May International Barbecue Cooking Contest, the Federal Express Porky Pilots of Memphis placed first in the whole hog category. Here are their tips for cooking the perfect pig:

(1.) Keep a low and constant fire. Cook with meat side down first, because it is heat sensitive. After turning the pig, you can cook at a higher temperature.

(2.) Place the coals directly under the hams and shoulders, the thickest pieces of meat.

(3.) A 130- to 150-pound pig should be started 20 to 24 hours before it is to be eaten. Cook meat side down for 7 hours before turning. Cook the remainder of the time with skin side down, which allows the skin to hold in the juices.

(4.) Baste every hour, when cooking meat side down. When cooking skin side down, baste every half hour.

(5.) Begin fire with hot bed of oak coals covered with ½-inch of moist persimmon sawdust. Put hickory chips on coals 1 hour before removing meat.

(6.) Baste with an oil and vinegar sauce seasoned with hot pepper, garlic, celery, beer, and salt. Serve with a ketchup-based dipping sauce.

Honey Pork Ribs

Ingredients for 4 servings:
4½ lbs. pork spareribs, cut into 1-rib
   lengths
½ cup honey
½ cup frozen orange juice concentrate,
   undiluted
Dijon-style mustard, for dipping

Directions:
Preheat oven to 350°. Arrange ribs in one
layer on rack in shallow roasting pan. Cover
pan tightly with foil. Bake 1 hour. Remove
ribs from rack. Pour off grease. Mix honey
and juice concentrate. Baste ribs with this
mixture. Grill over gray charcoals on barbecue grill until done, about 30-45 minutes
more. Serve hot, with mustard as a dipping
sauce.

Pork Chops Veracruz

Ingredients for 6 servings:
6 ¾-inch thick pork chops
1 Tbl. vegetable oil
1 Tbl. flour
1 Tbl. brown sugar
1 tsp. dry mustard
1 tsp. salt
1 clove garlic, mashed
2 medium onions, thinly sliced
1 cup dry white wine, divided in half
1 medium green pepper, seeded and
   chopped
2-3 Tbl. pimiento, coarsely chopped
1 4-oz. can chopped green chiles

Directions:
In heavy skillet, brown pork chops on both
sides in oil over medium-high heat. Drain
excess fat. Sprinkle with flour, brown sugar,
mustard, salt, and garlic. Add onion and ½
cup of the wine. Cover. Cook over low heat
until tender, about 1 hour. Add the other ½
cup wine, green pepper, pimiento, and chiles
15 minutes before chops are done.

Pork Chops Baked in Wine

Ingredients for 4 servings:
1 lb. fresh mushrooms, chopped
6 oz. Swiss cheese, shredded
½ cup fresh parsley, minced
1 tsp. seasoned salt
4 1-inch thick pork loin chops with pockets
½ cup flour
salt, to taste
black pepper, to taste
2 eggs, beaten
2 cups cracker crumbs
4 Tbl. vegetable oil
½ cup dry white wine
1 Tbl. flour
2-3 cups hot milk

Directions:
Combine mushrooms, cheese, and parsley. Add seasoned salt. Combine. Stuff mixture into pork chop pockets. Secure with wooden picks. Dip chops in ½ cup flour seasoned with salt and pepper, and then into beaten eggs. Dredge in cracker crumbs. Heat oil in large, heavy-bottomed skillet. Add chops. Brown on both sides. Drain oil from skillet. Add wine. Cover. Simmer 1 hour. Add more wine, if needed. Remove chops to platter, to keep warm. Add 1 Tbl. flour to drippings. Mix well. Gradually stir in milk. Season to taste with salt and pepper. Cook, stirring, until sauce is thick and very hot. Pour over chops or serve to the side. Serve with rice or mashed potatoes.

South Carolina-Style Barbecue

Ingredients for 6 to 8 servings:
1 3-4-lb. Boston butt pork roast
4 cloves garlic, peeled
1 cup cider vinegar
1 tsp. black pepper, freshly ground
water
2 cups cider vinegar
1 tsp. crushed red pepper flakes
1 tsp. salt

Ingredients for Simple Barbecue Sauce:
1 part tomato ketchup
1 part vinegar
1 part vegetable oil
black pepper, to taste
paprika, to taste

Directions:
Place pork in Dutch oven or heavy kettle with garlic, 1 cup vinegar, pepper, and water to cover. Bring to boil. Reduce heat. Partially cover. Simmer 2-2½ hours. Preheat oven to 350°. Drain pork. Place on rack in roasting pan. Bake 2 hours or until meat is very tender. Brush every 15 minutes with sauce made by combining 2 cups vinegar, red pepper flakes, and salt. Remove pork from oven. Serve with your favorite barbecue sauce or with Simple Barbecue Sauce.

Note:
You can vary the seasonings here, if they appear too hot. However, don't scrimp on the vinegar; it flavors the meat and tenderizes it, too.

Orange-Ginger Pork Roast

Ingredients for 10 to 12 servings:
1 tsp. dry mustard
1 tsp. salt
½ tsp. white pepper
½ tsp. ground ginger
3-4-lbs. boneless pork loin roast, rolled
   and tied

Ingredients for Glaze:
1 cup orange marmalade
¼ cup light corn syrup
2 Tbl. lemon juice
½ tsp. dry mustard
½ tsp. ground ginger

Directions:
Preheat oven to 325°. Combine dry mustard, salt, white pepper, and ginger. Mix well. Rub into pork roast. Place roast on rack in shallow roasting pan. Insert meat thermometer in thickest part of roast. Cook, uncovered 35-40 minutes per lb., or until meat thermometer reads 170°.

   Make glaze: Combine all ingredients in medium saucepan. Cook over medium heat 5 minutes, stirring often. Baste with glaze every 10 minutes during last 30 minutes cooking time. Let roast stand 10 minutes before carving, to allow juices to set.

Roast Pork with Cabbage

Ingredients for 8 servings:
1 4-6-lb. boneless pork loin roast
4 strips bacon, cut into 1-inch pieces
2 medium onions, sliced
1 garlic clove, minced
8 cups red cabbage, chopped
1 tsp. salt
1 tsp. crushed fennel
½ cup white wine

Directions:
Preheat oven to 325°. Place pork roast in open roasting pan. Insert meat thermometer in thickest part. Roast uncovered until thermometer reads 165°, about 1½ hours. Let sit 30 minutes after removing from oven. Meanwhile, fry bacon until crisp. Drain. Add onion and garlic to drippings. Sauté 2-3 minutes. Add remaining ingredients. Cover. Cook 10 minutes, or until cabbage is crisp-tender. Stir well. Sprinkle bacon over cabbage. Serve with pork along with buttered, parsleyed potatoes.

Note:
   Accompany this meal with a nice German Riesling wine, and you will have a feast.

Pork Chops with Herbs

Ingredients for 4 servings:
⅓ cup (generous) golden raisins
¾ cup dry vermouth
1 Tbl. unsalted butter
2 tsp. olive oil
4 8-oz. center-cut pork chops
¾ cup onions, thinly sliced and peeled
1½ tsp. thyme
1½ tsp. rosemary
½ tsp. salt
dash black pepper
zest of ½ orange, grated
1½-2 cups beef stock *or* bouillon
few sprigs fresh parsley
½ bay leaf

Directions:
Two nights before serving this dish, cover raisins in vermouth. Soak overnight.

The day before serving, add butter and oil to skillet. Brown pork chops evenly on both sides. Transfer to large baking dish in one layer. Preheat oven to 350°.

Cook onions in skillet in remaining fat until soft. Pound thyme and rosemary in mortar. Sprinkle over chops. Season with salt and pepper. Spread onion over all. Drain raisins, reserving vermouth.

Discard most of fat from skillet. Add vermouth to deglaze. Turn up heat. Add orange zest, raisins, and stock to pan. Stir for few minutes. Pour liquid over chops. Scatter parsley and bay leaf over all. Cover with aluminum foil. Bake 1 hour, or until meat is tender. Transfer chops to heat-proof dish. Remove bay leaf and parsley from sauce. Pour into saucepan. Simmer, until reduced to 2½ cups, skimming off fat. Reduce until slighty thicker. Pour back over chops. Refrigerate until day of dinner party. Before serving, cook, covered, at 350° for 30 minutes. Serve hot with zucchini soufflé and hot Parmesan bread.

Note:
From Anita Kidd for dinner party for 4 under $25.

Pork Medallions in Mustard Sauce

Ingredients for 4 servings:
8 2½-oz. medallions of pork
salt, to taste
pepper, to taste
flour
3-4 Tbl. vegetable oil
⅔ cup white wine
⅔ cup sour cream
1 tsp. Dijon-style mustard
¼ tsp. dried basil
1 hard-cooked egg, minced, for garnish

Directions:
Sprinkle pork with salt and pepper. Dust with flour. Heat oil in frying pan. Sauté pork for 4 minutes on each side, or until browned and cooked through. Transfer to heated serving platter. Add wine to pan. Bring to boil over high heat, stirring up browned bits. Reduce for 1 minute, then stir in sour cream. Heat mixture 2 minutes, or until thickened. Remove skillet from heat. Stir in mustard and basil. Serve medallions with sauce. Garnish with egg.

Note:
    From Anita Kidd of Atlanta, Georgia.

Sausage en Croute

Ingredients for 8 servings:
1 sheet frozen puff pastry
1 lb. mild Italian sausage
½ cup onion, chopped
⅓ cup green pepper, chopped
1 large tomato, chopped, peeled, and
    seeded
1 cup Swiss cheese, shredded
4 Tbl. parsley, chopped

Directions:
Preheat oven to 425°. Thaw puff pastry 20 minutes. Meanwhile brown sausage in skillet, stirring to break into bits. Add onion and green pepper. Cook until soft. Drain fat from sausage. Transfer to mixing bowl. Fold in tomato, cheese, and parsley. Unfold and roll out pastry to 10-by-14-inch rectangle on lightly floured board. Spread sausage mixture evenly over pastry. Roll up from the long side into "jelly roll." Transfer to baking sheet lined with brown paper. Pinch edges to seal and form circle. Pinch together. Cut at 2-inch intervals, ⅔ of the way down. Turn pieces up slightly, so cut edge can show. Bake 20 minutes.

Note:
    Delicious alongside pasta or with a simple salad. It freezes well, too.

Sausage-Stuffed Eggplant

Ingredients for 4 servings:
1 1½-lb. eggplant, sliced lengthwise into
 halves
2 Tbl. salt
1 lb. mild Italian sausage, casings
 removed and sausage crumbled
¾ cup onion, chopped
1 cup tomato purée
½ tsp. black pepper
½ tsp. dried oregano
½ cup water
½ tsp. salt
2 Tbl. feta cheese, crumbled
1 Tbl. parsley, minced
1 tsp. hot pepper sauce
2 Tbl. feta cheese, crumbled
2 Tbl. Parmesan cheese, grated

Directions:
Scoop out pulp of eggplant, leaving ½-inch
thick shell. Reserve pulp. Sprinkle shell with
2 Tbl. salt. Turn cut side down on paper
towels. Drain 45 minutes. Pat dry.
 Preheat oven to 375°. In heavy kettle or
stock pot, brown sausage. Add onions. Stir
and cook, until pork is evenly browned.
Drain off fat. Add tomato purée, black
pepper, oregano, water, and ½ tsp. salt to
sausage. Cook over medium heat 10 minutes, stirring occasionally. Cut eggplant pulp
into ½-inch cubes. Add to meat mixture.
Cook 15 minutes more. Remove sauce from
heat. Stir in 2 Tbl. feta cheese, parsley, and
hot pepper sauce. Spoon mixture into shells.
Place shells in greased, shallow baking dish.
Sprinkle with 2 Tbl. feta cheese and Parmesan cheese. Bake 45-50 minutes, or until
heated through.

Note:
 Quite a hearty entree. All you need is a
simple salad and good crusty bread to sop up
the juices.

Bebe's Country Ham

Ingredients:
1 country ham
cold water
1 cup vinegar
water
white sugar
brown sugar

Ingredients for Red-Eye Gravy:
ham drippings
½ cup strong coffee *or* water

Directions:
How to bake country ham: Saw the hock off any size ham and save it for cooking with black-eyed peas. Wash ham and place in a large container; cover with cold water, and soak for 12 hours. Add 1 cup vinegar to water. Preheat oven to 400°. Remove ham from water. Place ham in roasting pan, skin side up. Fill pan about half way up with cold water. Place top on roaster and put in oven to bake. As soon as ham starts baking, turn heat down to 325°, and cook 20 minutes per pound. When ham is done, remove from oven and remove skin from ham. Take ham from pan; discard grease. Place ham back in roasting pan and sprinkle with a mixture of half white and half brown sugars, depending on the size of ham. Put under the broiler until golden brown.

How to fry country ham: Slice ham and remove outside skin. Heat heavy-bottomed skillet and place ham in skillet. Cook until golden brown on one side, turn ham, turn heat to low, pour ½ cup water in skillet and cook just a short time, until done. Add more water if needed.

Note:
After frying ham, leave drippings in skillet and add ½ cup strong coffee. Stir and reduce over medium heat until gravy is reddish in color. The result is red-eye gravy.

Piccadillo

Ingredients for 8 servings:
2 medium onions, chopped
2 large green peppers, seeded and
  chopped
4 Tbl. vegetable oil, divided in half
1½ lbs. ground chuck, crumbled
½ tsp. celery salt
½ tsp. dried oregano
½ tsp. dried basil
¼ tsp. salt
½ tsp. black pepper
3 cloves garlic, minced
¼ tsp. cayenne pepper
29 oz. tomato sauce
1 Tbl. Worcestershire sauce
½ cup green olives, sliced, juice reserved
1 3-oz. jar capers, drained
1 cup raisins
reserved olive juice (optional)
almond slivers, toasted (optional)

Directions:
In large, heavy-bottomed skillet, place onions and peppers in 2 Tbl. oil. Sauté over medium heat until soft, about 8 minutes. Set aside. Add 2 Tbl. more oil to skillet. Add beef. Sauté meat, until it is browned. Add celery salt, oregano, basil, salt, black pepper, garlic, cayenne pepper, and reserved onions and peppers. Mix well. Add tomato sauce and Worcestershire sauce. Stir to blend. Cook 10 minutes over medium heat, so flavors will mingle. Stir occasionally. Add olives, capers, and raisins. Cook over low heat, covered, 40 minutes. Add reserved olive juice, if needed for consistency. Top with slivered toasted almonds.

Note:
Serve Piccadillo over yellow or white rice, or carry it to a tailgate picnic before the football game and stuff into pita bread pockets. Serve with an avocado salad and black beans for a full meal.

Elegant Beef in Red Wine Sauce

Ingredients for 4 servings:
4 6-oz. fillets of beef
salt, if desired
black pepper, freshly ground, to taste
1 tsp. peanut oil
3 Tbl. shallots, chopped
1 Tbl. butter
¾ cup dry red wine
1 Tbl. butter

Directions:
Flatten each fillet gently. Sprinkle on both sides with salt and pepper. Heat oil in heavy skillet. Add meat. Cook over moderately high heat 3 minutes. Turn. Cook 3 minutes. Turn once more. Cook 3 minutes for rare; turn again and cook 3 minutes for medium-rare. Total cooking time of 9-12 minutes is best. Transfer meat to warm platter. Pour fat from pan. Add shallots and 1 Tbl. butter. Cook, stirring, 30 seconds. Add wine. Bring to boil. Reduce heat. Cook 4 minutes, stirring up browned bits from skillet. Liquid should reduce to about ⅓ cup. Add 1 Tbl. butter. Blend well. Swirl sauce over fillets. Serve at once with roasted potatoes and a green salad.

Skillet Hamburgers with Cognac Sauce

Ingredients for 4 servings:
1 lb. ground chuck
2 tsp. Dijon-style mustard
2 Tbl. butter
1 cup heavy cream
½ cup cognac
black pepper, freshly ground, to taste

Directions:
Form beef into four patties. Paint both sides with mustard. Melt butter in large skillet. Sauté patties over medium heat 7 minutes on one side. Turn. Cook 7 minutes on the other (for rare burger). Remove patties to warm platter. Drain fat from skillet reserving brown bits clinging to bottom. Return pan to heat. Add cream and cognac. Stir constantly over medium-low heat, until sauce thickens and turns golden. Season with black pepper. Serve to the side or over patties.

Note:
    An easy way to dress up the mundane hamburger patty.

Seaside Beef and Broccoli Chow Mein

Ingredients for 4 to 6 servings:
1 ¾-lb. flank steak *or* round steak, cut
  diagonally into 1½-inch-by-¼-inch
  strips
2 Tbl. soy sauce
1 clove garlic, minced
1½ Tbl. cornstarch
¼ tsp. ground ginger
dash cayenne pepper
¼ cup dry sherry
1¼ cups beef broth
2 Tbl. peanut oil
¼ cup green onions, chopped
1 Tbl. peanut oil
½ lb. fresh bay scallops
2 Tbl. peanut oil
½ lb. fresh broccoli flowerets
2 Tbl. water
1 8½-oz. can sliced water chestnuts,
  drained
1 3-oz. can chow mein noodles

Directions:
In medium bowl, combine beef, soy sauce,
and garlic. Let stand at room temperature 15
minutes. In another bowl, combine cornstarch, ginger, cayenne pepper, sherry, and
beef broth. Set aside. In wok or large skillet
over high heat, heat 2 Tbl. oil. Add beef and
green onions. Stir-fry until light brown.
Remove meat. Add 1 Tbl. oil to wok. When
hot, add scallops. Stir-fry 1-2 minutes.
Remove scallops. Add 2 Tbl. oil to wok.

Heat until hot. Add broccoli. Stir-fry about 1
minute. Add water and water chestnuts.
Cover. Cook 3 minutes, or until broccoli is
tender. Add cornstarch mixture, meat, and
scallops. Stir-fry, until meat sauce thickens
and scallops are well heated. Arrange chow
mein noodles on serving platter. Pour
mixture over. Can also serve with fried or
boiled rice.

Note:
  From Sally Hughes of Dunwoody,
Georgia, winner of a Chun King cooking
contest in Atlanta in 1980.

Texas Beef Brisket

Ingredients for 20 servings:
1 8-10-lb. beef brisket
¼ cup dry red wine
¼ cup bourbon
1 12-oz. can beer
1 Tbl. molasses
¼ cup soy sauce
1 tsp. or more black pepper, freshly
   ground
1 Tbl. salt
5 cloves garlic, minced
2 medium onions, minced
2 ribs celery, minced
⅓ cup chopped canned green chiles
Flour tortillas

Directions:
Pat beef dry. Set aside. In glass bowl,
combine all ingredients, except chiles and
tortillas. Lay brisket on large piece of
heavy-duty foil. Spread marinade over.
Tightly wrap brisket in foil. Refrigerate to
marinate overnight. The next day, preheat
oven to 200° and open foil. Sprinkle on more
pepper. Reseal. Place wrapped brisket in
second foil wrapping. Place on jelly-roll pan
or in roasting pan. Bake 8 hours. Remove
pan from oven. Drain juices from meat and
reserve. After meat is slightly cooled, wrap
in clean sheet of foil. Reserve, or refrigerate
to serve chilled. Place drippings and leftover
marinade in saucepan with green chiles.

Reduce to half the amount over medium
heat. Serve brisket, sliced, with buttered
flour tortillas and reserved sauce.

Note:
   This was served as an hors d'oeuvre to a
meal of Kansas City-style and Mexican
foods. It goes a long way and should be
served with sauce.

Buttermilk Marinated Kebabs

Ingredients for 8 servings:
2-2½ lbs. beef chuck *or* round, cut into
    1-inch cubes
small yellow onions
water
green peppers, cut into 1-inch squares
water
cherry tomatoes
medium-sized fresh mushrooms

Ingredients for Marinade:
2 Tbl. packed brown sugar
2 Tbl. fresh lemon juice
1 Tbl. Worcestershire sauce
1½ tsp. salt
2 cups buttermilk

Directions:
Make marinade: Combine all ingredients
except buttermilk in shallow dish. Add
buttermilk. Blend well.

Add meat to marinade. Cover. Refrigerate 24 hours. Remove from refrigerator 1
hour before cooking.

Prepare kebabs: Parboil onions in boiling water to cover 7 minutes. Rinse in cold
water. Drain. Parboil green pepper squares
in boiling water 2 minutes. Rinse in cold
water. Drain.

Assemble kebabs: Alternate pieces of
meat, and onions, green pepper, tomatoes,
and mushrooms on skewers. Brush kebabs
with marinade. Grill over hot coals, turning
every 5 minutes, until meat reaches right
degree of doneness. Allow about 12 minutes
for medium-done meat.

Note:
These kebabs also can be broiled. Place
4-6 inches under broiler. Cook 12-14 minutes, turning throughout cooking time.
Brush with marinade; the buttermilk tenderizes the meat.

Simple Pot Roast

Ingredients for 6 to 8 servings:
flour, as needed
salt, to taste
pepper, to taste
1 4-5-lb. boneless bottom round roast of
   beef, tied
3 Tbl. vegetable oil
2½ cups beef broth
½ cup dry red wine
2 Tbl. tomato paste
6 medium onions, peeled and halved
2 ribs celery, halved
2 bay leaves
4 medium potatoes, quartered
4 carrots, quartered
3 Tbl. flour
⅓ cup cold water
pan drippings reserved from roast
salt, to taste
pepper, to taste
watercress *or* parsley, as garnish

Directions:
Rub flour, salt, and pepper into all sides of
roast. Heat oil in heavy Dutch oven. Brown
meat on all sides over high heat. Combine
broth, wine, and tomato paste; pour over
roast. Add onions, celery, and bay leaves.
Bring mixture to boil. Cover. Reduce heat.
Simmer 2-2½ hours, until meat is just
tender. Add potatoes and carrots. Cook
15-20 minutes longer, until vegetables are
just tender. Transfer roast to platter; sur-
round with vegetables. Cover. Keep warm.
Whisk 3 Tbl. flour into cold water to blend.
Gradually whisk into broth and drippings
from meat. Bring to boil. Stir. Simmer until
thick. Taste. Add more salt and pepper, if
needed. Snip ties from roast. Slice. Serve
with gravy. Serve with more steamed vegetables, if desired. Garnish with fresh watercress or parsley.

Cold Marinated Eye of the Round

Ingredients for 12 servings:
2 cups dry red wine
3 shallots, minced
5 sprigs parsley
1 Tbl. Dijon-style mustard
2 Tbl. mixed fresh herbs, minced (chives, tarragon, rosemary)
4 Tbl. vegetable oil
salt, to taste
pepper, to taste
1 3-4-lb. eye of the round roast

Directions:
In small mixing bowl, blend all ingredients, except roast. Place beef in separate bowl. Pour marinade over. Cover well. Place in refrigerator overnight, or let stand at room temperature 8 hours. When ready to cook, remove meat from marinade. Place in roasting pan. Heat oven to 450°. Cook beef 10 minutes on 1 side. Salt and pepper lightly. Turn. Cook 10 minutes on other side. Remove from pan for a rare roast. Let cool. Serve or wrap, refrigerate, and serve chilled. Serve plain or with your favorite sauce.

Note:
An eye of the round roast is an affordable alternative to beef tenderloin.

George's Jerky

Ingredients:
1 1½-2-lb. beef flank steak
½ cup soy sauce
¼ tsp. garlic salt
¼ tsp. lemon-pepper seasoning
¼ cup red wine

Directions:
Trim all visible fat from meat. Cut meat along grain into thin strips, no more than ¼-inch thick. Combine remaining ingredients. Place beef in glass dish. Pour marinade over. Cover. Marinate 12 hours in refrigerator.

Place beef on racks atop cookie sheets. Bake at 150° 10-12 hours. Beef should be dry, but not crisp. Store in airtight jars at room temperature.

Note:
From George Goldman, an Atlanta commercial realtor who is active in scouting and hiking. Known for his trail concoctions — a backpacking gourmet.

Marinated Flank Steak

Ingredients for 4 servings:
1½ cups beer
3 green onions, minced
⅓ cup olive oil
3 Tbl. soy sauce
2 Tbl. sugar
1 Tbl. ginger root, peeled and grated
2 large cloves garlic, minced
1 tsp. salt
¼ tsp. Tabasco sauce
1½ lbs. beef flank steak

Directions:
Combine all ingredients, except flank steak, in small bowl. Whisk well. Place steak in ceramic or glass dish. Pour marinade over. Cover. Marinate in refrigerator 2 days, turning occasionally. Broil 2 inches under broiler or on grill over glowing coals 3-4 minutes per side. Thinly slice on the diagonal.

Note:
    Try this marinade on 'most any roast or tough cut of beef.

Grilled Chuck Roast

Ingredients for 6 to 8 servings:
1 4-5 lb., 2 inches thick beef chuck roast
½ cup vegetable oil
½ cup red wine vinegar
2 Tbl. Worcestershire sauce
2 large cloves garlic, minced
1 tsp. dried basil
4-5 peppercorns, crushed

Directions:
Pierce roast with fork. Place in plastic bag in shallow pan. Stir together remaining ingredients, except peppercorns. Pour over meat. Seal bag. Chill, turning meat occasionally, at least 4 hours, preferably overnight. Lift meat from marinade. Spread crushed peppercorns out on flat surface. Press meat in pepper, coating both sides. Place meat on greased grill 4-6 inches above solid bed of glowing coals. Turn once, basting with reserved marinade until meat is done to your liking, 30-40 minutes for rare. To serve, cut meat across grain in thin, slanting slices.

Note:
    The marinade tenderizes the beef and imparts a special flavor.

Sautéed Veal Scallops with Morel Sauce

Ingredients for 4 servings:
2 lbs. boneless veal loin, skinned and
    trimmed of fat
2 Tbl. vegetable oil
6 Tbl. unsalted butter
salt, to taste
ground white pepper, to taste
2 Tbl. fresh chives, chopped, for garnish

Ingredients for Morel Sauce:
2 oz. fresh morels *or* 1 oz. dried morels
water
1 Tbl. unsalted butter
1 Tbl. shallots, finely chopped
1 cup dry white wine
1 cup cognac
3 cups heavy cream
3 Tbl. unsalted butter
salt, to taste
ground white pepper, to taste

Directions:
Make sauce: Rinse dried morels under cold water until free of dirt. Transfer to bowl. Cover with cold water. Soak 2 hours. Drain. Rinse. Set aside. Cut very large morels into halves. If morels are fresh, wipe with damp paper towel. Cut off stems for other use. Slice large mushroom caps into halves. Set aside.

Melt 1 Tbl. butter in large skillet. Sauté shallots about 2 minutes. Add morels. Heat thoroughly. Add wine and cognac. Heat on high, until liquid has reduced to 1 cup. Add cream. Reduce liquid on high to half the amount. Add 3 Tbl. butter. Whip with wire whisk, until sauce is thickened. Lower heat. Add salt and white pepper. Reserve sauce.

Prepare veal: Cut loin into 1½-oz. medallions. Pound between pieces of wax paper to ¼-inch thickness. Heat oil in heavy skillet. Add butter. Melt. Add veal slices, a few at a time. Season with salt and pepper. Sauté quickly, about 30 seconds per side, or until lightly browned. Place scallops on serving platter. Spoon heated sauce over veal. Top with chives.

Note:
From Trotters Restaurant in Atlanta. Morels, of course, are wild mushrooms.

Veal Scallops with Lemon

Ingredients for 6 servings:
1 lb. veal, cut into ⅛-inch thick slices
2 eggs, lightly beaten
¾ cup flour
salt, to taste
pepper, to taste
2 Tbl. vegetable oil
2 Tbl. butter
2 Tbl. butter
juice of 1 lemon
2 Tbl. fresh parsley, chopped
1 lemon, seeded and sliced into rings, for
  garnish

Directions:
Dip veal scallops into egg. Dredge in flour seasoned with salt and pepper. Brown veal on both sides in oil and 2 Tbl. butter, heated in large or electric skillet. Remove to platter, to keep warm. Add 2 Tbl. butter to small skillet. When bubbling, add lemon juice and parsley. Pour sauce over veal. Garnish with lemon slices.

Note:
    Once in a while, we all deserve a splurge meal. Mine would be veal with hot, buttered pasta to the side.

Lamb Chops in Foil

Ingredients for 4 servings:
4 1½ inches thick lamb chops
1 small eggplant, peeled and sliced
1 large onion, sliced
2 medium tomatoes, halved
1 green pepper, seeded and sliced
dried basil, to taste
salt, to taste
pepper, to taste
2 cloves garlic, minced

Directions:
Preheat oven to 350°. Place each lamp chop in large square of aluminum foil. On each chop place eggplant slice, onion slices, tomato half, and green pepper slices. Sprinkle each with basil, salt, pepper, and minced garlic. Seal packs well. Place on baking sheet. Bake about 30 minutes for medium-rare.

Note:
    Foil is the answer to no-mess cooking. Use same procedure for salmon steaks, hamburger patties, or boneless chicken breasts. You will need to add a pat of butter to foil packs containing fish or chicken, however.

Grilled Leg of Lamb

Ingredients for 6 to 8 servings:
1 8-oz. jar Dijon-style mustard
2 tsp. crushed rosemary
2 tsp. fresh ginger root, chopped
1 clove garlic, crushed
3 Tbl. soy sauce
3 Tbl. peanut oil
1 5-7-lb. leg of lamb, boned and flattened

Directions:
In glass dish large enough to fit lamb, mix mustard, rosemary, ginger, garlic, soy sauce, and oil. Add lamb. Marinate overnight, turning after 1 hour.

Remove lamb from marinade. Place on hot grill over gray coals. Cook 10-15 minutes on each side, depending on size of lamb. Part will be well-done, part medium-done, and part rare. This can also be broiled. Baste during cooking with marinade. Slice lamb on the diagonal. Serve with assorted vegetables, grilled alongside lamb.

Note:
A favorite recipe from Atlanta's fine cooking teacher, Nathalie Dupree.

Venison Meatloaf

Ingredients for 6 to 8 servings:
2 lbs. ground venison
¼ lb. mild pork sausage
1 large onion, chopped
1 small green pepper, seeded and chopped
1 6-oz. can tomato paste
3 ribs celery, chopped
¼ cup dry red wine
½ tsp. dried thyme, crumbled
2 eggs, beaten
¼ cup chili sauce
2 tsp. butter, melted
1 cup dry bread crumbs
salt, to taste
pepper, to taste

Directions:
Preheat oven to 400°. In large mixing bowl, combine all ingredients. Place mixture in well-greased 9-by-5-by-3-inch casserole dish. Bake 1 hour, 15 minutes.

Note:
This is a good way to present venison to the entire family.

Venison Scallopini

Ingredients for 6 servings:
2 lbs. venison loin, cut into ¼-inch thick
   slices
2 eggs, beaten
1¼ tsp. salt
½ tsp. black pepper, freshly ground
⅓ cup flour
⅓ cup bread crumbs
½ cup butter
2 lemons, cut into wedges, for garnish
3 Tbl. parsley, chopped, for garnish

Directions:
With meat mallet or dull edge of French
knife, pound venison to ⅛-inch thickness,
turning once. In shallow baking pan, combine eggs, salt, and pepper. Place flour in
another shallow pan. In third shallow pan,
place bread crumbs.

   Coat venison medallions in flour. Dip in
eggs and coat well with crumbs. In 12-inch
skillet, melt butter. Cook venison over
medium heat 3-4 minutes per side, or until
browned. Remove to warm platter. Garnish
with lemon and parsley.

Note:
   Too often, people overcook and overseason wild game. This recipe brings out the
venison's natural flavor.

Fried Rabbit

Ingredients for 4 to 6 servings:
2 rabbits, cut up
salted cold water
salt, to taste
black pepper, to taste
garlic powder, to taste
2 eggs
½ cup flour
¾ cup dry bread crumbs
vegetable oil, for frying
½ cup water

Directions:
Cup up rabbits; soak in salted cold water 20
minutes. Drain well. Add salt, black pepper,
and garlic powder to eggs in small bowl. Mix
well. Dip rabbit pieces in egg mixture and
then into flour. Dip again in egg and then
into bread crumbs. Place rabbit pieces on
platter. Cover and refrigerate until 30
minutes before cooking. Allow rabbit to
come to room temperature. Pour oil to
¼-inch depth in large frying pan. Brown
rabbit in hot oil on both sides, until golden.
Pour ½ cup water into pan. Cover. Reduce
heat to simmer. Cook rabbit 25 minutes
more. Remove cover. Cook another 10
minutes, or until the crust is crisp.

Note:
   Rabbit is lower in fat and calories than
veal, turkey, lamb, beef, or pork, and it
contains more protein, the U.S. Department
of Agriculture reports.

Vegetables

A Mess of Greens

In the South, you don't go out and purchase a bunch of spinach or kale; you go out and buy a "mess of greens."

Greens is quite a generic term here, describing chard, kale, mustard, collards, spinach, poke sallet, and turnip greens — all similar but each with its own flavor.

As a general rule, select young greens when possible. They take less time to cook than older plants, and they're more tender. Southerners prepare their greens with a piece of pork (usually ham hocks, bacon, or salt pork), not to make the greens taste greasy, but to season them. They should need only a grinding of black pepper, a touch of vinegar, or a dab of pickled hot peppers for completion. During hard economic times, greens and beans were flavored with meat, so that they tasted like meat and could take its place on the table.

All greens should be washed well, several times, in changes of water to remove dirt and sand before cooking. Remove stems and drain well.

When preparing chard and spinach, place the greens in a pot without water and slowly cook them until the water in the greens comes out — usually less than 30 minutes. Season with salt, pepper, melted butter, and cheese, if desired. Mustard greens most often are prepared mixed with turnip greens.

To prepare turnip greens, wash well and drain. Place ½ to 1 pound ham hock to every 5 pounds greens in a pot with 2 quarts water. Simmer 45 minutes and then add greens. Cook an additional 45 minutes or until greens are tender. It's best to cook the meat for greens first before adding them to the pot.

Collards should boil with plenty of water and can be served with tiny new potatoes, boiled, to the side.

Hearty Potato Casserole

Ingredients for 4 servings:
6 slices bacon
1 Tbl. bacon fat, reserved from bacon
2 cups onion, chopped
4 eggs, beaten
½ cup dry bread crumbs
½ tsp. salt
½ tsp. black pepper
4 medium unpeeled potatoes, grated
1½ cups Swiss cheese, shredded
paprika

Directions:
Preheat oven to 350°. Fry bacon in skillet, until crisp. Drain well. Reserve 1 Tbl. bacon fat. Add onions to skillet. Cook about 8 minutes over low heat, until soft. In mixing bowl, combine eggs, bread crumbs, salt, and pepper. Mix well. Stir in onions and potatoes. Pour mixture into buttered, shallow 6-cup baking dish. Crumble bacon on top. Distribute cheese over bacon. Dust with paprika. Bake 20-30 minutes.

Note:
   Delicious at brunch or on a chilly Sunday night with a tossed salad and red wine.

Quick Stuffed Potatoes

Ingredients for 4 servings:
4 baking potatoes
4 Tbl. butter
¼ cup plain, low-fat yogurt
1 tsp. salt
⅛ tsp. black pepper
¼ cup Cheddar cheese, shredded

Directions:
Bake potatoes at 425° about 50 minutes, or until centers are soft. Cut thin slice lengthwise from top of each potato. Scoop out pulp, reserving shells. Mash pulp with butter, yogurt, salt, and pepper in mixing bowl. Spoon back into shells. Smooth tops. Sprinkle with cheese, patting it down. Return potatoes to oven. Bake until cheese melts and insides are hot, about 10 minutes.

Note:
   These freeze well. After topping with cheese, wrap for freezing. To reheat, unwrap and place on baking sheet. Bake at 425° 45-60 minutes.

Phyllis' Sweet Potato Soufflé (page 122)

Vidalia Onion Rings (page 132)

Potato au Gratin

Ingredients for 6 servings:
6 white potatoes, peeled and sliced
   ¼-inch thick
3 onions, sliced into thin rings
salt, to taste
black pepper, freshly ground, to taste
3 cups Gruyere (*or* any good Swiss)
   cheese, shredded
3 cups milk

Directions:
Preheat oven to 350°. Layer potatoes and onions in greased, 2½-quart casserole. Sprinkle each layer with salt, pepper, and cheese. Pour milk over all. Cover. Bake 30 minutes. Remove cover. Bake another 30 minutes, or until potatoes are easily pierced and the top is golden and crusty.

Note:
   Country French and so good.

Potatoes Roquefort

Ingredients for 6 servings:
6 baking potatoes
½ cup Roquefort *or* blue cheese
heavy cream
salt, to taste
black pepper, freshly ground, to taste
⅓ cup dry bread crumbs
1 clove garlic, mashed
3 Tbl. butter, melted

Directions:
Bake scrubbed potatoes in 350° oven 1 hour, or until easily pierced. Slice off tops. Scoop out pulp. Reserve shells. Mash potato pulp or press through ricer. Beat in cheese. Gradually beat in cream, until potato mixture is light and fluffy. Season with salt and pepper. Spoon potato mixture into reserved shells, heaping filling high. In bowl, mix bread crumbs, garlic, and butter. Sprinkle mixture over potatoes. Bake in 350° oven 20-25 minutes, or until brown and crusty.

Note:
   Can be prepared ahead and then baked.

Phyllis' Sweet Potato Soufflé

Ingredients for 8 servings:
3 cups sweet potatoes, cooked and
    mashed
1 cup sugar
¼ cup milk
2 eggs
1 tsp. vanilla extract
½ cup butter, melted
⅓ cup flour
1 tsp. orange peel, grated
2 Tbl. orange juice concentrate, diluted,
    or fresh orange juice

Ingredients for topping:
1 cup pecans, chopped
1 cup brown sugar
½ cup butter, melted
⅓ cup flour

Directions:
Preheat oven to 350°. In mixing bowl,
combine all ingredients, except topping
ingredients. Pour into greased baking dish.
Combine all topping ingredients in small
bowl. Scatter over sweet potato mixture.
Bake 40 minutes.

Note:
   Sweet potatoes are a Southern ingre-
dient, but this recipe comes from a Midwes-
tern source — Phyllis Singer of Waterloo,
Iowa.

Tomato Pudding

Ingredients for 6 to 8 servings:
2 cups tomato purée
½ tsp. salt
1 cup packed brown sugar
½ cup boiling water
4 slices white bread, toasted and cubed
½ cup butter, melted

Directions:
Preheat oven to 350°. Combine tomato
purée, salt, brown sugar, and water in bowl.
Mix well. In an 8-inch, shallow baking pan,
place toast cubes. Pour melted butter over.
Top with tomato mixture. Bake at 350° for 30
minutes.

Note:
   A very sweet vegetable dish, this pudding could take the place of sweet potato
casseroles at holiday dinners.

Oven-Fried Green Tomatoes

Ingredients for 6 servings:
½ cup yellow cornmeal
½ tsp. salt
¼ tsp. black pepper
1 egg
1 Tbl. water
3 medium-sized green tomatoes, cut into
  ¼-inch thick slices
vegetable cooking spray *or* butter, melted

Directions:
Preheat oven to 450°. Combine cornmeal, salt, and pepper in bowl. Set aside. Beat egg and water together. Set aside. Dip tomato slices first in egg mixture. Dredge in cornmeal mixture to coat. Lightly spray 10-by-15-inch baking pan with vegetable spray or spread lightly with melted butter. Use only enough butter to keep tomatoes from sticking. Place tomatoes in single layer in pan. Bake 30-40 minutes, or until golden brown. Turn halfway during cooking.

Note:
  From Corene Love of the Fulton County (Georgia) Extension Service, who says slices of zucchini squash or yellow squash can be prepared the same way.

Eggplant with Fresh Tomatoes

Ingredients for 6 servings:
1 1½-lb. eggplant, peeled and cut into
  ¼-inch thick slices
boiling water
2 Tbl. butter
2 eggs, beaten
¼ tsp. black pepper
1 Tbl. onion, chopped
½ tsp. dried oregano
⅓ cup saltine cracker crumbs
8-10 fresh tomato slices, peeled
½ cup shredded Monterey jack *or*
  Cheddar cheese

Directions:
Preheat oven to 375°. Place eggplant in saucepan with ½-inch boiling water. Cover. Cook about 10 minutes, or until eggplant is tender. Drain. Mash.
  Turn eggplant into mixing bowl. Add butter, eggs, pepper, onion, oregano, and cracker crumbs. Taste for seasoning; add salt, if needed. Turn into buttered, 1-quart casserole. Cover with tomato slices. Sprinkle cheese on top. Bake 25 minutes, or until light brown.

Note:
  Lighter than an Eggplant Parmesan.

Basil-Stuffed Tomatoes

Ingredients for 4 servings:
4 large tomatoes
2 Tbl. soft bread crumbs
1 tsp. Parmesan cheese, grated
1 tsp. butter
2 tsp. fresh basil, chopped

Directions:
Preheat oven to 350°. Remove cores and stems from tomatoes, leaving hollows in centers. Mix remaining ingredients. Fill center of each tomato with quarter of stuffing. Bake 45 minutes.

Pan-Fried Eggplant

Ingredients for 4 to 6 servings:
1 medium eggplant, peeled and halved
   lengthwise
1 egg, slightly beaten
1 Tbl. water
½ cup rich, round crackers, crushed
2 Tbl. parsley, minced
salt, to taste
pepper, to taste
½ cup vegetable oil

Directions:
Cut eggplant halves crosswise into ½-inch slices. Combine egg and water. In separate bowl, combine cracker crumbs, parsley, salt, and pepper. Dip eggplant into egg mixture. Coat with crumb mixture on both sides. Heat oil in large frying pan. When hot, add eggplant slices, a few at a time. Cook about 2-3 minutes per side, turning once, until golden. Drain on paper towels or absorbent brown paper.

Note:
   This procedure works well for zucchini and yellow crookneck squash, too.

Eggplant Timbale

Ingredients for 8 servings:
1 large *or* 2 medium eggplants
1½ cups Parmesan cheese, grated
2 eggs, lightly beaten
6 Tbl. butter, melted and cooled
½ cup fresh tomatoes, chopped (optional)
¼ cup parsley, minced
¼ tsp. salt
black pepper, freshly ground, to taste
2 Tbl. Parmesan cheese, grated
¾ cup dry bread crumbs
butter (optional)

Directions:
In boiling water in large saucepan, cook eggplant 30 minutes, or until tender. Drain. Peel. Preheat oven to 375°. Mash pulp in mixing bowl with 1½ cups Parmesan cheese, eggs, and butter. Stir in chopped tomatoes, if desired, parsley, salt, and pepper. Blend well. Spoon mixture into lightly buttered, 1½-quart casserole. Sprinkle top with 2 Tbl. Parmesan cheese, bread crumbs, and more butter if desired. Bake 30 minutes, or until set.

Note:
   Can be made ahead and baked at the last minute.

Shrimp-Stuffed Eggplant

Ingredients for 4 servings:
1 1¼-lb. eggplant, cut lengthwise into halves
water
¼ cup mushrooms, sliced
½ cup onions, chopped
¼ cup butter, melted
1 tsp. salt
⅛ tsp. black pepper
1 lb. shrimp, shelled, cleaned, and cooked
2 Tbl. dry bread crumbs
1 Tbl. Parmesan cheese, grated

Directions:
Preheat oven to 375°. Scoop out pulp of eggplant, leaving ½-inch shell. Parboil shells 5 minutes. Drain. Reserve. Chop pulp. Sauté with mushrooms and onions in butter over medium heat 10 minutes, stirring occasionally. Mix in salt, pepper, and shrimp. Pile into eggplant shells. Sprinkle with bread crumbs and cheese. Bake 25 minutes.

South-of-the-Border Squash

Ingredients for 6 to 8 servings:
1½ lbs. summer squash (zucchini *or* yellow)
1 medium onion, chopped
2 Tbl. butter
1 4-oz. can diced green chilies, drained
2 Tbl. flour
1 tsp. salt
½ tsp. black pepper
1½ cups Monterey jack cheese, shredded
1 egg
1 cup cottage cheese
2 Tbl. parsley, chopped
½ cup Parmesan cheese, grated

Directions:
Preheat oven to 400°. Dice squash. Sauté with onion in butter, until tender but crisp. Fold in chilies, flour, salt, and pepper. Pour into greased, 2-quart baking dish. Sprinkle with Monterey jack cheese. Combine egg, cottage cheese, and parsley. Layer over cheese. Sprinkle with Parmesan cheese. Bake uncovered 25-30 minutes, or until heated through.

Note:
From Anne Downs of Statham, one winner in the Homemade Good News publication recipe contest, spring, 1983.

Stuffed Acorn Squash

Ingredients for 4 servings:
2 medium-sized acorn squash, split lengthwise down the middle
vegetable oil

Ingredients for apple filling:
2 medium-sized cooking apples, chopped
½ cup onion, chopped
3 Tbl. butter
2 cups cottage cheese
juice of 1 lemon
dash cinnamon
¾ cup Cheddar cheese, shredded
¼ cup walnuts, chopped *or* raisins (optional)

Directions:
Preheat oven to 350°. Remove seeds from squash. Bake, face down on oiled tray, 30 minutes.

Make apple filling. Sauté apples and onion in butter, until onion is clear. In mixing bowl, combine apples and onions with remaining filling ingredients. Stuff into squash cavities.

Bake, covered, 15-20 minutes, or until mixture is heated through.

Squash-Sausage Casserole

Ingredients for 4 to 6 servings:
6-8 medium-sized yellow summer squash, sliced
2 medium onions, sliced
water
1 lb. pork sausage
1 cup Cheddar cheese, shredded
2 eggs
1 5.3-oz. can evaporated milk
½ tsp. salt
½ tsp. black pepper, freshly ground
⅛ tsp. nutmeg, freshly grated
⅓ cup dry bread crumbs

Directions:
Preheat oven to 350°. Place squash and onions in saucepan with small amount of water. Cover. Cook until tender. Drain. (This should be about 4 cups squash and onions.) Meanwhile, break up sausage in frying pan. Cook until done, but not browned. Drain. Mash squash mixture. Place half of squash and half of meat in greased casserole. Add half of cheese. Mix eggs, milk, salt, pepper, and nutmeg. Pour half of egg mixture over cheese. Add remaining squash and sausage. Add remaining egg mixture. Add remaining cheese. Top with bread crumbs. Bake 25-35 minutes.

Note:
Try spicy sausage for a change of pace.

Snow Peas with Water Chestnuts

Ingredients for 4 servings:
2 cups fresh snow peas
2 Tbl. vegetable oil
½ cup water chestnuts, sliced
½ cup sliced bamboo shoots
½ tsp. sugar
½ tsp. salt
½ tsp. salt (optional)

Directions:
String pea pods. If pods are long, cut into 2-3 pieces about 1 inch long. Rinse. Drain. Set wok or heavy skillet over high heat. When hot, add oil. Add water chestnuts and bamboo shoots. Mix a few times. Add sugar and ½ tsp. salt. Mix again. Add snow peas. Stir-fry quickly, just heating them through. Add more salt, if desired. Mix again. Serve at once.

Note:
From Deen Terry of Atlanta, the best Chinese cooking instructor around.

Turnip au Gratin

Ingredients for 4 servings:
1 clove garlic
3 Tbl. butter
1½ lbs. turnips, peeled and thinly sliced
½ tsp. salt
black pepper, freshly ground, to taste
1 tsp. dried herb mixture
3 oz. ham, sliced into thin strips
3 oz. Swiss cheese, thinly sliced
½ cup heavy cream
¼ cup dry bread crumbs

Directions:
Preheat oven to 400°. Rub small casserole dish well with cut garlic clove. Let dry. Butter dish well. Reserve remaining butter for topping. Arrange turnip slices, slightly overlapping, in 3 layers. Sprinkle salt, pepper, herbs, and ham between the 2 intermediate layers. Arrange slices of cheese on surface. Pour cream over. Sprinkle with bread crumbs. Top with reserved butter. Bake 45 minutes.

Note:
    Serve alongside turnip greens, if you like.

Fresh Corn Pudding

Ingredients for 4 servings:
10 ears corn, yellow *or* white
2 Tbl. onion, minced
2 Tbl. minced green bell *or* red bell
    pepper
1½ tsp. salt
1¾ cups half-and-half

Directions:
Preheat oven to 350°. Husk corn. With sharp knife, split kernels, cutting down the ears lengthwise. With back of knife, scrape out kernels. With edge of knife, cut kernels from cob into mixing bowl. Add remaining ingredients. Mix well. Pour into greased, 1½-quart casserole. Bake 1 hour. Serve hot with butter, sliced tomatoes, country-fried steaks, and cold beer.

Note:
    The corn must be fresh. Add milk according to the milkiness of your corn.

Winter Corn Pudding

Ingredients for 6 servings:
2 Tbl. butter
2 Tbl. onion, minced
2 Tbl. flour
2 Tbl. light brown sugar
1 cup milk
2 eggs
½ tsp. salt
¼-½ tsp. white pepper
¼ tsp. nutmeg
1 16-17-oz. can whole-kernel corn, drained

Directions:
Preheat oven to 325°. In saucepan, melt butter. Add onion. Cook until soft. Stir in flour and sugar until smooth. Take pan off heat. Whisk in milk. Return to heat. Cook, stirring, over low heat, until thick and boiling. Remove from heat. In small bowl, beat eggs wth salt, pepper, and nutmeg, until foamy. Quickly stir ¼ cup sauce into egg mixture. Stir all egg mixture back into sauce. Stir in corn. Turn into buttered, 1-quart casserole. Place in pan of water that comes as high as corn mixture. Bake 50-60 minutes.

Note:
When you can't buy fresh corn, this can be an adequate substitute.

Roasted Corn

Ingredients:
yellow *or* white corn, in husks
iced, salted water
melted Herb Butter (see page 190)

Directions:
Pull tops of corn husks down. Remove corn silks. Replace husks. Soak corn in iced, salted water 45 minutes. Place corn in husks on grill. Roast for about 10 minutes. Turn. Roast 10 minutes. Serve with melted Herb Butter.

Curried Corn with Peppers

Ingredients for 4 servings:
3 ears yellow corn
3 large sweet peppers, at least one red *or* yellow
2 Tbl. butter
1 onion, finely chopped
salt, to taste
pepper, to taste
1 Tbl. good quality curry powder
½ cup heavy cream

Directions:
Cut kernels from corn. You should have about 1½ cups. Set aside. Core and seed peppers. Slice into thin julienne strips. You should have about 4 cups. Heat butter in heavy skillet. Add onion. Cook, stirring, until soft and translucent, about 3 minutes. Add pepper strips, salt, and pepper. Cook 1 minute. Sprinkle with curry powder. Stir to blend. Cover. Cook on low heat for 5 minutes, stirring often. Add corn. Stir well. Add cream. Cook just 1 minute more.

Fresh Spinach au Gratin

Ingredients for 4 servings:
1 bunch fresh spinach, about 10 oz.
1 Tbl. olive oil
1 cup soft bread crumbs
½ cup Swiss cheese, shredded
salt, to taste
black pepper, freshly ground, to taste
1½ Tbl. olive oil

Directions:
Preheat oven to 450°. Rinse spinach several times, to remove sand. Set aside to drain. Brush bottom and sides of 1-quart casserole or au gratin dish with 1 Tbl. olive oil. Pile handful of spinach at time on chopping board. Chop leaves. Press spinach into dish. Top with bread crumbs, cheese, salt, and pepper. Drizzle top with 1½ Tbl. olive oil. Bake 10 minutes. Reduce heat to 350°. Cook 10-15 minutes more.

Green Beans à la Basquaise

Ingredients for 6 servings:
1 lb. slender green beans
salted water
ice water
¼ cup olive oil
1 dried chile pepper, halved
6 tomatoes, peeled, seeded, and chopped
¼ cup parsley, finely minced
4 large basil leaves, minced
2 cloves garlic, minced
½ tsp. dried thyme *or* 1 sprig fresh
   thyme
½ tsp. dried oregano *or* 2 sprigs fresh
   oregano
salt, to taste
black pepper, freshly ground, to taste
fresh parsley, minced, for garnish
Parmesan cheese, grated, for garnish

Directions:
Snap off ends of beans, leaving beans whole. Rinse. Drain well. Bring salted water to boil in 6-8-quart pan. Add beans. Cook 5-7 minutes until tender-crisp. Drain in colander. Plunge at once into ice water. Set aside.

Heat oil in heavy skillet over high heat. Add chile pepper. Cook until darkened. Discard pepper. Add remaining ingredients, except garnish. Bring to boil. Reduce heat. Simmer, partially covered, 30-45 minutes, or until tomato liquid has evaporated and sauce is thick. Remove cover after 25 minutes, if too much liquid remains.

Stir in green beans. Cover. Simmer 5-10 minutes, or until heated through. Taste and correct seasoning. Garnish with parsley and Parmesan cheese. For a main course, add diced smoked ham.

Note:
From Anita Kidd, accomplished Atlanta chef.

The tomato sauce can be made a day ahead and reheated. Serve with grilled flank steak and a simple onion custard for fall or winter meal. Or serve as a main dish in summertime.

Green Beans with Cumin

Ingredients for 4 servings:
¾ lb. tender fresh green beans
water
salt, to taste
1 Tbl. butter
juice of ½ lemon
¼ tsp. ground cumin
2 Tbl. fresh parsley, chopped
black pepper, freshly ground, to taste

Directions:
Pull off ends of beans. Rinse. Drain. Place in saucepan. Add cold water to cover and salt. Bring to boil. Reduce heat. Simmer 5-6 minutes, or until tender. Drain.

Add remaining ingredients. Toss to blend, while cooking quickly over high heat, about 10 seconds.

Note:
A Southern vegetable seasoned well. The cumin is an alternative to bacon or ham hocks.

Vidalia Onion Rings

Ingredients for 4 servings:
1¼ cups flour
¼ tsp. salt
1 egg, slightly beaten
1¼ cups milk
1 tsp. vegetable oil
5 large Vidalia onions, peeled and cut into ¼-inch thick slices
vegetable oil, for frying

Directions:
In mixing bowl, combine flour and salt. Add egg, milk, and oil. Blend well with wooden spoon. Batter will be slightly lumpy. Separate onions into rings. Dip in batter. Drop a few at a time into deep fryer or wok filled with at least 6 inches cooking oil heated to 375°. Cook until rings are golden brown and rise to surface, about 1-2 minutes. Drain on paper towels.

Green Onion au Gratin

Ingredients for 4 servings:
5 bunches green onions
1 Tbl. butter
salt, to taste
black pepper, to taste
2 Tbl. butter
¾ cup fresh bread crumbs
½ cup Parmesan cheese *or* Romano
cheese, grated
1 egg
½ cup half-and-half

Directions:
Preheat oven to 375°. Trim green onions of roots and 3 inches of stems. Cut on the diagonal into 1-inch pieces. In large frying pan, toss onions with 1 Tbl. butter over high heat 1-2 minutes, or until soft. Arrange onions in buttered, 1½-quart dish. Season well with salt and pepper.

To same skillet, add 2 Tbl. butter. Heat until foaming. Add bread crumbs. Stir. Cook over medium heat, until crumbs are golden, about 3 minutes. Mix bread crumbs wtih cheese. Beat egg with half-and-half. Pour over onions. Top with crumb-cheese mixture. Bake about 20-25 minutes, or until golden.

Note:
When a generous neighbor kept providing me with green onions from his garden, I came up with this recipe.

Stir-Fry Asparagus

Ingredients for 4 to 6 servings:
2 lbs. fresh asparagus
¼ cup butter *or* margarine
½ tsp. salt
⅛ tsp. black pepper
½ tsp. dried thyme

Directions:
Wash asparagus. Snap off ends as far down as they break easily. Cut on the diagonal into 2-inch pieces. Melt butter in large skillet. Add asparagus. Sprinkle with seasonings. Cover. Cook over medium high heat about 5 minutes, stirring occasionally, until lower part of stalk is just crisp-tender.

Note:
An excellent accompaniment to any poultry or beef dish.

Betty's Fried Okra

Ingredients for 4 servings:
1 lb. okra
salted ice water
yellow cornmeal
salt, to taste
black pepper, freshly ground, to taste
oil, for deep frying

Directions:
Wash okra well. Trim caps. Slice into ½-inch pieces. Soak 15 minutes in salted ice water. Drain. While deep fat is heating to 350°, roll okra in cornmeal seasoned with salt and pepper. Dredge only a few at a time, making sure to coat each piece well. Drop small batch at a time into hot fat. Fry until okra floats on surface and is crispy golden brown. Remove from fat with slotted spoon. Drain on paper towels or absorbent brown paper. To keep okra warm while frying batches, place in single layer on baking sheets lined with paper towels. Place baking sheets in warm oven.

Note:
　　Betty Spence of Albany, Georgia, prepared this for lunch during a cooking class at Rich's in Atlanta, and everyone went back for more.

Honey-Glazed Carrots

Ingredients for 4 servings:
1 lb. carrots, peeled and cut on the
　　diagonal into slices
water
salt, to taste
4 Tbl. honey
juice of 2 lemons

Directions:
Slice carrots. Place in saucepan of cold water to cover. Salt to taste. Bring to boil, then cook about 5 minutes, or until just tender. Drain. Combine with honey and lemon juice.

Note:
　　Carrots taste better with honey.

Pasta, Beans & Grains

Truly Grits

When yankees are down South, they ask for grits at breakfast. Southerners don't ask — they just expect them.

And they expect them properly cooked: not lumpy, not cold, and certainly not of a "quick-cooking" or "instant" variety, for heaven's sake.

Grits, coarsely ground dry white corn, is that porridge-like cereal that is boiled and served for breakfast or folded into casseroles or soufflés.

Grits are to Southern cooking what rice is to Oriental fare and pasta to the Italian cook. They are as much a part of our culinary heritage as crab stew and sweetened iced tea.

The reason many folks don't like grits (as hard to understand as that may be) is that they haven't eaten true grits. These are grits cooked slowly over low heat and stirred often so they don't stick to the saucepan. And if they do stick, any good cook knows to turn the pan under water and let it sit a while — the grits will unstick themselves.

Grits are easy to cook if you follow package directions. Quick-cooking or instant grits don't have the holding capacity of regular grits; they must be served up fast from the pot. Ordinary grits can be cooked and then set in a double boiler over warm water before time to serve.

Grits are delicious topped with butter, grated cheese, or with traditional red-eye gravy.

Grits Soufflé

Ingredients for 6 servings:
butter
1 cup milk
1 cup water
2 tsp. salt
½ cup grits
4 Tbl. unsalted butter
¼ tsp. black pepper, freshly ground
1 clove garlic, crushed
dash cayenne pepper
1 cup sharp Cheddar cheese, shredded
3 egg yolks, lightly beaten
9 egg whites
¼ tsp. cream of tartar

Directions:
Preheat oven to 350°. Butter 2-quart soufflé dish. Set aside. Combine milk, water, and salt in saucepan. Bring almost to boil. Add grits, stirring. Reduce heat. Simmer about 5 minutes, or until mixture thickens. Remove from heat. Add 4 Tbl. butter, pepper, garlic, cayenne pepper, and cheese. Mix well, until butter has melted. Add beaten egg yolks. Mix well. Set aside.

Beat egg whites until stiff. Beat in cream of tartar. Add ⅓ egg white to batter. Fold in gently. Add remaining egg white. Fold until well combined. Pour batter into soufflé dish. Place dish on top of cookie sheet on middle shelf of oven. Bake 30-40 minutes, or until mixture has puffed.

Note:
A beautiful brunch dish when served along with sliced, fried country ham or sausage, fresh fruit, and your choice of home-baked breads.

ᔰ Melody's Pesto Sauce on Pasta (page 186)

Apple Upside Down Cake (page 154)

Fried Grits

Ingredients:
grits
1 egg, beaten with 1 tsp. water *or* milk
dry bread crumbs
salt, to taste
pepper, to taste
butter *or* bacon drippings

Directions:
Prepare grits of any variety — regular, quick-cooking or instant. Pour grits into a loaf pan, glass or square dish and allow to cool, covered, until set. Leave in refrigerator overnight. Cut grits into ½-inch thick slices. Dip in beaten egg, mixed with a little milk or water, and roll in dry bread crumbs that have been seasoned with salt and pepper. In a heavy skillet, melt butter or bacon drippings over moderate-high heat and add grits slices. Brown on both sides and around the edges. Serve with grilled or roasted poultry, with ham and eggs for breakfast or instead of hush puppies with fish.

Note:
For leftover grits — should there be any.

Fried Rice

Ingredients for 2 to 4 servings:
1-2 Tbl. vegetable oil
1-2 green onions, chopped
1 small clove garlic, minced
1 tsp. fresh ginger root, grated
1-2 cups cold rice, cooked
cooked meat *or* vegetables *or* mixture of
    both, chopped
1 Tbl. soy sauce
1 egg, lightly beaten

Directions:
Heat oil in wok or large, heavy skillet. Add green onion, garlic, and ginger. Stir-fry over medium heat 1 minute. Add rice, a handful of meat, and soy sauce. Stir-fry, stirring and tossing, to prevent rice from sticking, 2-3 minutes. Add beaten egg. Stir until egg is set and mixed throughout rice.

Note:
Fried rice can be made with leftover cooked shrimp, crab, fish, chicken, steak, pork, and 'most any chopped, cooked vegetable.

Daisy Young's Red Beans and Rice

Ingredients for 8 servings:
1 lb. dry red beans
water to cover, for soaking
2 ham hocks
3 medium onions, chopped
2 ribs celery, chopped
2 green peppers, seeded and chopped
3 cloves garlic, minced
2 bay leaves
water (optional)
salt, to taste
pepper, to taste
½ cup butter
cooked rice

Directions:
Pick over beans. Cover with water in large bowl to soak overnight. The next day, drain beans. Place in large kettle or stock pot with ham hocks, onions, celery, green pepper, garlic, and bay leaves. Cover with cold water. Cover with lid. Bring to boil. Reduce heat. Simmer about 2½-3 hours, adding more water if needed to keep beans from sticking. Remove 2 cups beans (or more, if you desire a thicker consistency) from pot. Mash. Return mashed beans to pot. Stir well. Season well with salt and pepper. Add butter. Heat until butter has melted. Serve hot with cooked rice.

Note:
    Daisy Fuller Young is the mother of Atlanta's mayor Andrew Young. When she comes to Atlanta from her home in New Orleans for Christmas, she prepares this dish — a tradition on Christmas Eve.

Spicy Rice Pilaf

Ingredients for 4 servings:
1 Tbl. butter
1 Tbl. vegetable oil
1 small onion, thinly sliced
2 cloves garlic, minced
½ tsp. tumeric
¼ tsp. cinnamon
½ tsp. cumin seeds
½ tsp. salt
½ tsp. black pepper
dash cayenne pepper
1 cup uncooked rice
1 cup beef *or* chicken broth
1 cup water
½-1 cup cooked chicken, diced *or* shrimp
   or cooked and drained ground beef,
   pork, *or* lamb
1 cup frozen peas, thawed

Directions:
In large skillet, heat butter and oil. Add onion. Sauté over medium heat about 8 minutes, or until onion is translucent and golden. Turn off heat. Add garlic, tumeric, cinnamon, cumin, salt, black pepper, and cayenne pepper. Stir in rice, coating well with spices.

Stir in broth, water, and meat (except shrimp, which should be added with peas). Bring to boil. Cover. Simmer over low heat about 10 minutes. Stir in peas (and shrimp). Simmer 5 minutes, or until rice has absorbed all liquid. Let sit, covered, 5 minutes before serving.

Note:
A spicy, Indian dish, this can accompany any grilled meats, or it can stand alone as the entree with a salad.

Black Beans and Rice

Ingredients for 8 servings:
1 lb. black beans
6 cups water
½ cup olive oil
1 cup onion, chopped
1 green pepper, seeded and chopped
2 cloves garlic, minced
2 tsp. salt
½ tsp. black pepper, freshly ground
1 1-lb. smoked ham hock
¼ cup red wine vinegar
4 cups cooked white *or* yellow rice
3 hard-cooked eggs, cut into wedges, for
  garnish
1 red onion, sliced into rings, for garnish
hot pepper sauce, to taste

Directions:
Wash beans. Place in large saucepan. Cover
with 6 cups water. Bring to boil.

In skillet, heat olive oil. Sauté onion,
green pepper, and garlic 5 minutes over low
heat, or until soft. Add to beans, along with
salt, pepper, ham hock, and vinegar. Bring
to boil. Lower heat. Cover. Simmer until
tender, about 3 hours, depending on age of
beans.

When beans are almost cooked, remove
ham hock. Allow to cool. Shred meat from
bone. Return to pot. To serve, spoon beans
over rice. Garnish with egg and onion.
Season to taste with hot pepper sauce.

Note:
This dish was inspired by a visit to Key
West, where only white rice is served under
these beans. I prefer the yellow rice.

Mushroom Rice

Ingredients for 2 servings:
1 cup chicken stock
½ cup uncooked rice
¼ cup fresh mushrooms, chopped
2 green onions, chopped
¼ cup pine nuts, chopped
salt, to taste
black pepper, to taste

Directions:
In 2-3-quart saucepan, bring stock to boil. Stir in remaining ingredients. Bring back to boil. Cover. Reduce heat. Simmer 20 minutes. Serve with lamb or beef kebabs.

Note:
    This recipe can be doubled or tripled easily. The pine nuts are especially good with lamb.

Savannah Red Rice

Ingredients for 10 servings:
½ lb. bacon
pan drippings reserved from bacon
¾ cup onion, chopped
2 16-oz. cans tomatoes, undrained
3 tsp. salt
½ tsp. black pepper
dash hot pepper sauce
2 cups uncooked rice

Directions:
Preheat oven to 350°. Fry bacon in large, cast-iron skillet with lid. When crisp, remove bacon from pan. Drain. Crumble. Set aside. Sauté onion in drippings. When soft, add tomatoes, salt, pepper, hot sauce, and bacon. Stir. Bring to boil. Add rice. Reduce heat. Stir. Cover securely. Cook 10 minutes on top of stove. Transfer pan to oven. Bake 40 minutes, or until rice is soft and liquid absorbed. Serve as side dish to 'most any entree, or with gumbo.

Curried Rice

Ingredients for 4 to 6 servings:
1 Tbl. butter
⅓ cup onion, finely chopped
1 clove garlic, minced
1 Tbl. curry powder
1 bay leaf
salt, to taste
black pepper, freshly ground, to taste
1 cup uncooked rice
1½ cups chicken stock

Directions:
Heat butter in saucepan. Add onion and garlic. Cook, stirring, until soft. Add remaining ingredients, except stock, stirring to coat grains. Add broth. Cover. Bring to boil. Reduce heat. Cook 15-20 minutes. Remove bay leaf. Serve with any grilled or roasted meats.

Note:
Curry adds color and flavor to rice.

Vidalia Onion-Rice Casserole

Ingredients for 8 servings:
3 lbs. Vidalia onions, thinly sliced
½ cup butter
1 cup uncooked rice
2 cups water
1½ cups Swiss cheese, shredded
1⅓ cups half-and-half

Directions:
Preheat oven to 325°. Sauté onions in butter in large skillet until soft, about 10 minutes. Boil rice in water in saucepan 5 minutes. Drain well. Place onions, rice, cheese, and half-and-half in greased, 10-by-13-inch casserole. Bake, uncovered, 1 hour.

Note:
The casserole's flavor improves when assembled and baked in advance. Simply reheat at 325° for about 20 minutes.

Pasta with Garlic, Herbs, and Pine Nuts

Ingredients for 4 servings:
1 lb. spaghetti
6 Tbl. olive oil
3 Tbl. fresh garlic, minced
½ cup green onions, minced
¾ cup fresh basil, minced
¾ cup fresh parsely, minced
¼ tsp. black pepper, freshly ground
1 tsp. salt
2 Tbl. butter
½ cup Parmesan cheese
½ cup pine nuts, toasted
Parmesan cheese (optional)

Directions:
Cook spaghetti until firm, yet tender, about 10-12 minutes. Drain in colander. While spaghetti is cooking, heat oil in saucepan. Sauté garlic and green onions, until garlic begins to change color. Add basil, parsley, pepper, and salt. Pour over pasta. Toss to coat well. Add butter and Parmesan cheese. Toss. Portion pasta into individual bowls. Top each with about 2 Tbl. pine nuts and more cheese, if desired.

Note:
From Elaine Reader. Can vary with freshly steamed asparagus, snow peas, or mushrooms.

Black-Eyed Peas

Ingredients for 6 servings:
1 lb. dry black-eyed peas
5-6 cups water
1 small ham hock
2 tsp. salt
black pepper, freshly ground, to taste
1 large onion, chopped
1 fresh hot pepper, minced or dried, crumbled with seeds
1-2 cloves garlic, minced

Directions:
Place beans in colander. Rinse well with cold water. Drain. Place in heavy, 6-8-quart stock pot or kettle. Cover with water. Soak 12 hours or overnight. The next day, add ham hock and more water to cover, if needed. Bring peas to boil. Reduce heat. Add salt and pepper. Add onion, hot pepper, and garlic. Cover pot. Simmer 1-2 hours, or until peas are tender. Don't stir during cooking or you will break peas.

Note:
Serve with cooked turnip greens and hot cornbread on New Year's Day.

Saffron Rissoto

Ingredients for 8 servings:
2 Tbl. onion, minced
3 Tbl. butter
4½ cups water
3 beef bouillon cubes
½ tsp. powdered saffron
2 cups rice
1 cup frozen peas, thawed
¼ cup smoked ham, diced
3 Tbl. fresh basil, chopped *or* 2 tsp. dried basil mixed with 2 Tbl. fresh parsley, chopped
¼ cup Parmesan cheese, freshly grated
6 Tbl. butter
¾ cup Parmesan cheese

Directions:
Sauté onion in 3 Tbl. butter in large saucepan or 10-inch skillet until tender, but not brown. Heat water and bouillon cubes to boiling in saucepan. Dissolve saffron in ½ cup of hot broth. Add rice to onion in skillet. Sauté over low heat 2 minutes. Add broth and saffron. Cover. Cook 20 minutes. Remove from heat. Stir in peas, ham, and basil. Add ¼ cup Parmesan cheese and 6 Tbl. butter. Let stand, covered, about 5 minutes, or until all liquid is absorbed. Serve with ¾ cup Parmesan cheese.

Note:
    This recipe is from Jo Bettoja, a native of South Georgia who lives in Italy and runs the Lo Scaldavivande cooking school outside of Rome. Serve with any roasted beef or fowl, grilled meats, or especially, veal. For late-night suppers, serve as a main course along with a tossed salad and light vinaigrette dressing.

Fettuccine with Tomato Cream

Ingredients for 6 to 8 servings:
2 cups heavy cream
2¼ cups milk
4 Tbl. butter
4 medium ribs celery, cut into 3-inch
    lengths and then into matchstick
    julienne strips
2 large leeks, white part only, cut into
    3-inch julienne strips
2 large carrots, scraped and cut into
    3-inch julienne strips
lightly salted water
1 lb. spinach fettuccine *or* plain fettuccine
4 medium tomatoes, peeled, seeded, and
    cut into strips
salt, to taste
black pepper, freshly ground, to taste
about ¾ cup Parmesan cheese

Directions:
In heavy-bottomed saucepan, bring cream
and milk to boil. Reduce heat. Simmer until
reduced to ½ the original volume, about 30
minutes.

Meanwhile, melt butter in medium-sized
skillet. Add celery, leeks, and carrots. Cook
slowly, stirring often, until vegetables are
crisp-tender, about 5-6 minutes.

In large pot, bring lightly salted water to
boil. Add pasta. Boil rapidly, until just
tender, about 6 minutes. Drain pasta.
Return to pot. Add reduced cream, vegetable mixture, and tomatoes. Season with salt
and pepper. Toss, until all is well coated.
Toss in Parmesan cheese. Mix again. Serve
at once.

Note:
Although this pasta dish is a meal in
itself, it is an excellent accompaniment to
sautéed veal or chicken breasts.

Fettuccine with Mushrooms

Ingredients for 2 servings:
½ lb. mushrooms (button, ceps, or
   chanterelles)
4 Tbl. butter
2 Tbl. vegetable oil
2 cloves garlic, crushed
2 Tbl. shallots, minced
¼ cup dry white wine
½ cup heavy cream
salt, to taste
black pepper, freshly ground, to taste
8 oz. fettuccine
fresh parsley, chopped

Directions:
Rinse mushrooms. Pat dry. Thinly slice. In
heavy skillet, heat butter and oil. Sauté
garlic and shallots 2 minutes. Add mushrooms. Stir-fry 5 minutes. Add wine, cream,
salt, and pepper. Bring to simmer. Cook 2
minutes.

   Cook fettuccine in boiling water until
just tender. Drain. Place in heated bowl.
Pour sauce over. Sprinkle with parsley.

Note:
   A most satisfying Sunday supper for 2.
Add wine for a romantic meal.

Cakes

Baking a Pound Cake

Unadulterated is the word that comes to mind when I think of pound cake. Simple, unblemished, without frosting, and much to-do, the pound cake has risen to great heights in Southern cookery, and nationwide, for that matter.

But in the South, you will find that pound cakes are acceptable at most any occasion. Whether they're topped with spring strawberries or smothered in a caramel sauce during the holidays, pound cakes are the answer to the "What will I serve for dessert?" question. They are at home on picnics, tailgates, or even silver-service occasions.

The original pound cakes were just what the name suggests — a pound of sugar, pound of butter, pound of eggs, and pound of flour. Through the years, we have modified this recipe for economy's sake and because we can produce a lighter cake by making some changes, such as the addition of buttermilk and baking soda. More flavor is brought in with sour cream or a dash of almond extract.

When making any butter cakes, you should cream the butter thoroughly, until it is soft and fluffy, to incorporate air. Add sugar gradually and continue to cream until fluffy. This is a task, but since many recipes don't call for baking powder, it is the air in this mixture that will cause your cake to rise.

Eggs and butter both should be at room temperature before beginning. A pound cake is best baked in a cold oven, that is, placing the cake in the oven and then setting the temperature. A hot oven causes the cake to bake at the edge, stick to the pan, and not rise at the sides, thus rising in the center. A cool oven lets the cake rise with the heat of the oven, and therefore the cake will bake level.

In spite of numerous variations of the pound cake, such as butter pecan and chocolate and lemon sour cream, I believe the best pound cake is the most simple. There is no need to frost a cake so rich. If you must tamper with it, slice, toast, and top with butter or sweetened whipped cream.

Pumpkin Cake

Ingredients for 8 to 10 servings:
2 cups sugar
1 16-oz. can pumpkin
1 cup vegetable oil
4 eggs, beaten
2 cups flour
1 tsp. salt
2 tsp. baking soda
2 tsp. baking powder
2 tsp. ground cinnamon
½ cup flaked coconut
½ cup pecans, chopped

Ingredients for frosting:
½ cup butter, softened
1 8-oz. package cream cheese, softened
1 16-oz. package confectioners' sugar
2 tsp. vanilla extract
½ cup pecans, chopped
½ cup flaked coconut

Directions:
Preheat oven to 350°. Combine sugar, pumpkin, oil, and eggs in large mixing bowl. Beat at medium speed of electric mixer 1 minute. Combine flour, salt, baking soda, baking powder, and cinnamon. Add to pumpkin mixture. Beat 1 minute at medium speed. Stir in coconut and pecans. Pour into 3 greased and floured 8-inch round cake pans. Bake 25-30 minutes, or until cakes test done. Cool in pans 10 minutes. Remove from pans. Cool completely.

Make frosting: Combine butter and cream cheese. Beat until light and fluffy. Add confectioners' sugar and vanilla extract, mixing well. Stir in pecans and coconut.

Spread frosting between layers and on top of cake.

Note:
From Carole Moore, Atlantan, on the dessert sideboard at a Victorian Christmas party.

Sour Cream Coffee Cake

Ingredients for 2 9-by-5-by-3-inch loaves:
½ cup butter, softened
1 cup sugar
2 eggs, beaten
1 tsp. lemon juice
1 cup sour cream
2 cups sifted flour
½ tsp. salt
1 tsp. baking soda
1 heaping tsp. baking powder
1 tsp. vanilla extract

Ingredients for topping:
½ cup sugar
½ cup pecans, ground *or* walnuts, ground
2 tsp. cinnamon

Directions:
Preheat oven to 300°. Cream butter and sugar in large mixing bowl. Slowly add eggs. Incorporate well. Stir lemon juice into sour cream. Combine dry ingredients. Beginning and ending with dry ingredients, alternately add dry ingredients and sour cream-lemon juice mixture to batter. When well combined, add vanilla extract. Mix. Grease and flour two 9-by-5-by-3-inch loaf pans.

Make topping: Combine all topping ingredients.

Sprinkle 1 tsp. topping into each loaf pan, smoothing across bottom of pan. Pour ¼ of batter into each loaf pan. Scatter with more topping. Pour remaining batter into pans. Distribute remaining topping over tops. Bake 1 hour.

Note:
This cake is scrumptious served with coffee before midday and even better as a dessert. Keeps well and is a pretty gift any time of the year.

Hot Prune Cake

Ingredients for 12 servings:
1½ cups sugar
1 cup vegetable oil
3 eggs
1½ cups flour
1 tsp. salt
1 tsp. baking soda
1 tsp. cinnamon
1 tsp. nutmeg
1 tsp. allspice
1 cup buttermilk
1 tsp. vanilla extract
1 cup cooked prunes, chopped

Ingredients for topping:
1 cup sugar
½ cup buttermilk
½ tsp. baking soda
1 Tbl. white corn syrup
6 Tbl. butter
½ tsp. vanilla extract

Directions:
Preheat oven to 350°. Cream sugar and vegetable oil in large bowl with electric mixer. Add eggs, 1 at a time, beating well after each addition. Combine dry ingredients in separate bowl. Add dry ingredients to batter alternately with buttermilk. Begin and end with dry ingredients. Stir in vanilla extract and chopped prunes. Pour batter into greased and floured 9-by-13-by-2-inch baking pan. Bake about 30 minutes. Leave in pan.

Make topping: Combine all topping ingredients in top of double boiler. Cook, stirring, over low heat, until thick. Pour topping over cake while cake is still hot.

Sour Cream Chocolate Cake

Ingredients for 8 to 10 servings:
4 oz. unsweetened chocolate
½ cup margarine
2 cups sugar
2 eggs
¾ cup sour cream
2 cups flour
¾ tsp. salt
1½ tsp. baking soda
½ tsp. baking powder
1 cup water

Ingredients for Sour Cream Chocolate
    Frosting:
½ cup butter, softened
½ cup margarine, softened
4½ cups confectioners' sugar
6-8 oz. semisweet chocolate, melted and
    cooled
¾ cup sour cream
2 Tbl. vanilla extract

Directions:
Preheat oven to 350°. Melt chocolate and margarine in top of double boiler. Cool. Beat sugar and eggs in large bowl with electric mixer, until light. Add chocolate mixture, along with sour cream. Blend well. Sift together dry ingredients in separate bowl. Add to batter alternately with water. Begin and end with dry ingredients. Mix just to blend. Pour batter into 2 greased and floured 8-inch cake pans. Bake 30-40 minutes. Completely cool cake.

Make Sour Cream Chocolate Frosting: Cream butter and margarine. Add sugar. Beat until light. Add chocolate, sour cream, and vanilla extract. Beat, until light and fluffy.

Frost tops of layers and sides with frosting.

Jimmy's
Burnt Caramel Cake

Ingredients for 18 to 24 servings:
2 cups butter, softened
4 cups sugar
8 egg yolks
4 tsp. baking powder
6 cups sifted flour
2 scant cups milk *or* water
1 tsp. vanilla extract
1 tsp. lemon extract
8 egg whites

Ingredients for conserve:
½ cup peach preserves
¼ cup orange marmalade
¼ cup pecans, chopped

Ingredients for frosting:
¾ cup sugar
4¼ cups sugar
1 5½-oz. can evaporated milk
½ cup butter
1 tsp. vanilla extract
½ tsp. baking soda

Directions:
Preheat oven to 350°. Make cake: Cream butter, sugar, and egg yolks together in large mixing bowl. Beat until light and fluffy. Sift baking powder with flour. Add to mixture alternately with milk. Begin and end with dry ingredients. Add lemon and vanilla extracts. Beat egg whites, until stiff. Fold into batter gently. Pour ½ batter into greased and floured 13-by-9-inch pan.

Make conserve: Mix ingredients.

Fold conserve into remaining batter. Pour into another greased and floured 13-by-9-inch pan. Bake about 30-40 minutes, or until cakes test done. Place pans on racks to cool.

Make frosting: Heat ¾ cup sugar in large, heavy-bottomed skillet over medium heat. Meanwhile, watching so sugar in skillet doesn't burn, mix 4¼ cups sugar with milk in 4-quart saucepan. Heat to vigorous boil. When sugar in skillet has turned rich amber color, add to sugar-milk mixture. (Beware, for mixture will flare up.) Heat to 230°-235°, stirring. Set aside. Add butter, vanilla extract, and soda. Stir. Let cool 10 minutes. Whip with portable mixer to expedite cooling.

Turn out cakes from pans. Place layer with conserve on board or serving platter. Spread quickly with some icing before it gets hard. Place second cake layer on top. Begin to ice sides and top of cake, adding more warm milk to thin, if necessary.

Note:
Jimmy Bentley of Atlanta says this recipe has been in his family more than 100 years. He fondly remembers eating it as a child.

Hummingbird Cake

Ingredients for 8 to 10 servings:
3 cups flour
2 cups sugar
1 tsp. salt
1 tsp. baking soda
1 tsp. ground cinnamon
3 eggs, beaten
1½ cups vegetable oil
1½ tsp. vanilla extract
1 8-oz. can crushed pineapple, undrained
1 cup walnuts, chopped
2 cups bananas, chopped
1 cup walnuts, chopped

Ingredients for Cream Cheese Frosting:
2 8-oz. packages cream cheese, softened
1 cup butter, softened *or* margarine,
  softened
2 16-oz. packages confectioners' sugar
2 tsp. vanilla extract

Directions:
Preheat oven to 350°. Combine dry ingre-dients in large bowl. Add eggs and oil, stirring until dry ingredients are moistened. *Do not* beat. Stir in vanilla extract, pineap-ple, 1 cup walnuts, and bananas. Spoon batter into 3 well-greased and floured 9-inch cake pans. Bake 25-30 minutes, or until test done. Cool in pans 10 minutes. Remove from pans. Cool.
  Make Cream Cheese Frosting: Combine cream cheese and butter. Beat until smooth.

Add sugar, beating until fluffy. Stir in vanilla extract. Frost between layers of cake, top, and sides. Sprinkle with 1 cup walnuts.

Note:
  So good, you'll hum when you taste it.

Apple Upside Down Cake

Ingredients for 1 9-inch round cake:
½ cup butter
½ cup light brown sugar
2 medium-sized apples, peeled, cored,
   and cut into ½-inch slices
2 eggs
⅔ cup sugar
⅓ cup apple juice
1 tsp. lemon extract
1 cup cake flour
½ tsp. baking powder

Directions:
Preheat oven to 350°. Place butter in 9-inch, round cake pan. Heat in oven until melted. Sprinkle in brown sugar. Stir, until well moistened. Arrange apple slices in pattern on top of sugar-butter mixture. Press apples firmly into mixture. Heat pan in oven until sugar starts to bubble. Set aside.

Beat eggs and sugar until light and fluffy. Gradually beat in apple juice and lemon extract. Sift flour and baking powder together. Add to mixture, stirring until smooth. Pour batter over apples. Bake 35-40 minutes, or until toothpick inserted in center comes out clean. Remove from oven. Invert on serving platter. Let pan stay over cake 5 minutes before removing.

Brown Sugar Sour Cream Pound Cake

Ingredients for 1 10-inch tube cake:
2 cups firmly packed light brown sugar
1 cup butter, softened
3 eggs
1 cup sour cream
2¼ cups flour
1 tsp. lemon peel, grated
1 tsp. vanilla extract
½ tsp. baking soda
½ tsp. salt

Ingredients for glaze:
1 cup confectioners' sugar
1-2 Tbl. fresh lemon juice

Directions:
Preheat oven to 325°. In mixing bowl, cream sugar and butter, until light and fluffy. Add eggs 1 at a time, beating after each addition. Fold in sour cream alternately with flour. Add remaining ingredients. Mix well. Pour batter into greased and floured 10-inch tube pan. Bake about 60-65 minutes, or until cake tests done. Cool in pan on wire rack 15 minutes. Remove from pan. Cool completely.

Make glaze: Combine sugar and lemon juice. Add more lemon juice if desired. Drizzle over cake.

Kentucky Butter Cake

Ingredients for 12 servings:
1 cup butter, softened
2 cups sugar
4 eggs, room temperature
3 cups flour
1 tsp. salt
1 tsp. baking powder
½ tsp. baking soda
2 tsp. vanilla extract
1 cup buttermilk

Ingredients for Rum Glaze:
1 cup sugar
¼ cup hot water
½ cup butter
3 Tbl. dark rum *or* 1 Tbl. rum flavoring

Directions:
Preheat oven to 325°. Grease bottom of 10-inch tube pan. In mixing bowl, cream butter. Gradually add sugar. Cream until light and fluffy. Add eggs, 1 at a time. Beat well after each addition. Add remaining ingredients. Blend until moistened. Mix on medium speed 2 minutes. Pour into pan. Bake 60 minutes, or until top springs back when lightly touched.

Make Rum Glaze: In small pan, place sugar, water, and butter. Stir and mix, until butter melts. Add rum. Mix well. Prick top of cake with fork. Pour hot sauce over warm cake. Cool completely before removing from pan.

Note:
The rum can be omitted from the glaze if desired. If so, substitute 1 Tbl. vanilla extract.

Mississippi Mud Cake

Ingredients for 12 servings:
2 cups sugar
1/3 cup cocoa
1½ cups butter, softened
4 eggs
1 tsp. vanilla extract
1½ cups flour
1⅓ cups flaked coconut
1½ cups pecans, chopped
1 7-oz. jar marshmallow creme

Ingredients for frosting:
1 lb. confectioners' sugar
1/3 cup cocoa
½ cup butter, softened
½ cup evaporated milk
1 tsp. vanilla extract

Directions:
Preheat oven to 350°. In mixing bowl, cream sugar, cocoa, and butter, until light and fluffy. Add eggs, one at a time. Add vanilla extract. Mix well. Stir in flour, coconut, and pecans. Pour into greased and floured 13-by-9-inch pan. Bake 40 minutes. When done, spread marshmallow creme over top. Cool before frosting.

Make frosting: Sift together confectioners' sugar and cocoa. Set aside. Cream butter in mixing bowl. Add sugar-cocoa mixture. Fold in evaporated milk and vanilla extract.

Note:
After visiting Memphis and seeing Mud Island, we should rename this Southern favorite, Mud Island Cake.

Mrs. Harvey's White Fruitcake

Ingredients for 5 lbs. fruitcake:
1 lb. candied cherries
1 lb. candied pineapple
4 cups pecans
¼ cup flour
1 cup butter
1 cup sugar
5 eggs
1¾ cups flour
½ tsp. baking powder
4 Tbl. lemon extract
2 Tbl. vanilla extract

Directions:
Chop fruit and nuts into medium-sized pieces. Dredge in about ¼ cup flour, to prevent sinking to bottom of cake during baking.

Cream butter and sugar together, until light and fluffy. Beat in eggs, 1 at a time, until light after each addition. Stir in 1¾ cups flour and baking powder. Add lemon and vanilla extracts. With hands, blend in fruit and nuts.

Grease 10-inch tube pan *or* 2 9-by-5-inch loaf pans. Line with heavy brown paper. Grease again. Pour batter into pans. Place in cold oven. Turn temperature to 250°. Bake 2 hours for 2 loaves or 2½ hours for tube pan. Cool in pan(s) on cake rack.

Note:
This favorite fruitcake recipe of Jean Thwaite of the *Atlanta Journal* and the *Atlanta Constitution* has appeared in those newspapers for many years during the Christmas season. Mrs. Harvey, according to Jean, was Lucile Plowden Harvey of Tampa, who went to school in Atlanta but has lived in Tampa most of her life. The recipe originally came from Plowden Hall in London, England. During World War II, Mrs. Harvey sent the cake to soldiers in thirteen foreign countries.

Pumpkin Cheesecake

Ingredients for 12 servings:
Ingredients for crust:
1½ cups graham cracker crumbs
⅓ cup ground almonds
½ tsp. ginger
½ tsp. cinnamon
⅓ cup butter, melted

Ingredients for filling:
4 8-oz. packages cream cheese
1¼ cups sugar
3 Tbl. cognac *or* brandy
1 tsp. ginger
1 tsp. cinnamon
½ tsp. nutmeg
4 eggs, room temperature
¼ cup heavy cream
1 cup cooked *or* canned pumpkin

Ingredients for topping:
2 cups sour cream
¼ cup sugar
1 Tbl. maple syrup
1 Tbl. cognac *or* brandy
¼ cup toasted almonds

  Make crust: Preheat oven to 425°.
Combine all crust ingredients. Press
into bottom of 10-inch springform pan.
Bake 10 minutes. Remove from oven.
Reduce temperature to 325°.

  Make filling: Beat cream cheese, until
smooth. Gradually add sugar. Beat
until light and fluffy. Add cognac,
ginger, cinnamon, and nutmeg. Blend
well. Add eggs, one at a time, beating
well after each addition. Add cream
and pumpkin. Mix well.
  Pour filling into crust. Bake 45
minutes. Turn off oven. Don't open
door for 1 hour. Remove cake from
oven.
  Make topping: Preheat oven to 425°.
Blend all ingredients, except almonds.
Spread over cake. Return to oven 10
minutes. Cool to room temperature 1
hour. Arrange almonds in ring around
cheesecake. Chill 3 hours before
removing from pan. Freezes well.

Capo's Walnut Cake

Ingredients for 12 servings:
3 eggs
1½ cups sugar
2 tsp. vanilla extract
pinch salt
1½ cups flour
2 tsp. baking powder
1½ cups heavy cream, whipped
1 cup walnuts, ground

Directions:
Preheat oven to 350°. Grease and flour tube or bundt pan. In mixing bowl, beat eggs. Gradually add sugar. Beat about 5 minutes, or until pale yellow and creamy. Add vanilla extract. Sift together dry ingredients. Sprinkle ½ of dry ingredients over eggs. Gently fold. Fold in whipped cream, walnuts, and remaining dry ingredients. Pour into prepared pan. Bake about 45-55 minutes, or until center of cake springs back when lightly touched.

Note:
From Linda Cappozoli, who, along with husband John, owns and operates the ever-popular Capo's Café in Atlanta's Virginia-Highland neighborhood.

Praline Cheesecake

Ingredients for 12 servings:
crust:
1½ cups graham cracker crumbs
½ cup butter, melted
½ cup sugar
1 tsp. cinnamon

Ingredients for filling:
2 lbs. cream cheese
3 eggs
1 tsp. vanilla extract
2 cups packed brown sugar
1 cup pecans, chopped
3 Tbl. flour

Directions:
Preheat oven to 350°. Make crust: Combine all ingredients. Press mixture into bottom and sides of 9-inch springform pan.

Make filling: Cream cream cheese, until smooth. Add eggs and vanilla extract. Beat until fluffy. Stir in brown sugar, nuts, and flour. Stir just to combine. Pour into crust. Bake 1 hour, 10 minutes. Cool well. Refrigerate.

Note:
From Holly Wulfing, chef at the Georgia Governor's Mansion in Atlanta.

Chocolate Seduction

Ingredients for 8 to 10 servings:
10 oz. semisweet chocolate, broken into
  pieces
½ cup butter, cut into 8 pieces
6 egg yolks, room temperature
¾ cup sugar
2 tsp. dark rum
½ tsp. vanilla extract
6 egg whites, room temperature
¼ cup sugar
1½ cups heavy cream, chilled
1½ Tbl. confectioners' sugar
confectioners' sugar

Directions:
Heat oven to 375°. Butter and flour 8-inch
springform pan. Set aside. Melt chocolate
and butter in double boiler over simmering
water. Keep warm. Beat egg yolks at high
speed. Gradually add ¾ cup sugar. Beat,
until yolks are pale yellow and thick. Add
chocolate mixture. Beat until smooth. Add
rum and vanilla extract. Beat to blend.

In medium bowl, beat egg whites, until
soft peaks form. Gradually beat in ¼ cup
sugar. Continue beating, until stiff peaks
form. Fold whites into chocolate mixture.
Pour batter into reserved pan. Smooth top.

Bake chocolate mixture 15 minutes.
Reduce oven to 350°. Bake another 15
minutes. Reduce oven to 250°. Bake no
more than 25 minutes. Turn off oven. Prop
oven door open. Keep cake in oven 25
minutes. Remove cake from oven. Cover
top with damp paper towel. Let stand 5
minutes. Remove towel. Let cake cool.
Press top of cake down to smooth top; it will
crack. Transfer cake to serving platter. Whip
cream in chilled bowl, adding 1½ Tbl.
confectioners' sugar, until soft peaks form.
Dust top of cake with confectioners' sugar.
Serve cake at room temperature with
whipped cream.

Note:
   This cake is rich — sure to please
chocoholics. The trick is not to overbake.

Basic Pound Cake

Ingredients for 1 10-inch tube cake *or* 2
  9-by-5-inch loaves:
2 cups butter, softened
4 cups sifted confectioners' sugar
6 eggs, room temperature
2 tsp. vanilla extract
1 tsp. almond extract
4 cups sifted cake flour
½ tsp. salt

Directions:
Preheat oven to 350°. Cream butter. Gradually beat in sugar. Continue beating until light and fluffy. Beat in eggs, 1 at a time, beating well after each addition. Blend in extracts. Combine flour and salt. Add to creamed mixture.

Pour batter into greased and floured 10-inch tube pan. Bake 65-70 minutes, or until cake tests done. Cool in pan on wire rack 15 minutes. Remove from pan. Cool completely.

Note:
This cake can also be baked in 2 greased and floured 9-by-5-inch loaf pans. Bake at 350° for 50-55 minutes.

Cola Cake

Ingredients for 12 servings:
2 cups flour
2 cups sugar
½ cup margarine
1 cup cola
3 Tbl. cocoa
½ cup buttermilk
2 eggs, beaten
1 tsp. baking soda
1 tsp. vanilla extract
1½ cups miniature marshmallows

Ingredients for frosting:
½ cup margarine
3 Tbl. cocoa
6 Tbl. cola
1 lb. confectioners' sugar
1 cup pecans, chopped *or* walnuts,
  chopped

Directions:
Preheat oven to 350°. Combine flour and sugar in large bowl of electric mixer. Heat margarine, cola, and cocoa in saucepan, until boiling. Pour over flour mixture. Combine. Add remaining ingredients. Beat well. Pour into greased and floured 13-by-9-inch baking pan. Bake 30-40 minutes. (Frost top while hot.)

Make frosting: Combine margarine, cocoa, and cola in saucepan. Bring to boil. Place sugar in small mixing bowl. When margarine mixture boils, pour it over immediately. Beat well. Add nuts. Spread over hot cake.

Pies

The Chess Pie

Like most cooks, I was baffled about how such a typically Southern pie got such a crazy name. So I did a little reading and interviewing and found there are a host of explanations for the name "chess pie."

Most folks agree that it was an English pie to begin with, but what has happened to it through the years is another story. The chess pie I know and love is really a vinegar pie, originating in Kentucky. The cider vinegar and cornmeal it contains cut the sweetness and contribute to its coarse texture. Most chess pies really are custard pies.

Beth Sparks of the *Winston-Salem Journal* said some people believe the pie got its name from the town Chester, England, or that "chess" is a bastardization of the word cheese; since lemon cheese pies are simply custard pies, containing no cheese at all, this makes sense. Others believe the name comes from an old saying, which claimed that chess pie could be made, from "anything in your chest" (pantry). And one last possible explanation for the name is that a cook, when asked what was in the pie, would answer, "Oh, 'jes' pie."

Chess pies vary from one Southern state to another. What you must remember in baking them is that you should just barely stir in the eggs. If you incorporate air, the pie will rise in the oven and fall when it comes out.

Like the pound cake, I prefer a chess pie plain, without chocolate and without lemon.

To Pre-Bake Pie Crusts

If your pie shell is to be baked without a filling, you must first prick the dough in the pan with a fork.

If desired, place dry beans on top of the crust so that it bakes evenly. Place in a 450° oven and bake about 10-15 minutes or until the crust is golden brown. Cool on a rack before filling.

Note:

If you're using dry beans when baking the crust, remove them after 8 minutes baking and continue baking.

Frances Baker's Pie Crust

Ingredients for 1 crust:
1½ cups flour
pinch salt
pinch sugar
½ cup vegetable shortening
3 Tbl. ice water

Directions:
In bowl of food processor, place flour, salt, and sugar. Process once to combine all. Chill shortening briefly — about 3 minutes in the freezer will do. Break shortening into bits. Distribute around steel blade in bowl. Process with 7 on-off pulses, until shortening is broken into dry ingredients well. Add ice water. Process with 7 more on-off pulses, or until dough forms ball. Roll out. Proceed with pie recipe. This recipe doubles well.

Note:
This is the flakiest, easiest pie pastry recipe I have found. Make several batches at one time and freeze. Frances Baker is an excellent Nashville, Tennessee, cook.

Cheddar Cheese Pastry (for apple pies)

Ingredients for 2 crusts:
½ cup vegetable shortening
1 cup Cheddar cheese, finely shredded
  (extra-sharp is best)
1¾ cups flour
1 tsp. salt
7-8 Tbl. ice water

Directions:
Chill shortening in freezer 5 minutes. With shredding blade in place in food processor, shred Cheddar cheese. Set aside. Fit steel blade into processor. Place flour and salt in work bowl. Process with a pulse. Add cheese. Process with another pulse. Add chilled shortening, cut into tiny pieces. Process about 10 seconds, or until mixture resembles large peas. Add a little water. Process about 5 seconds, adding more water if needed. Process another 5 seconds, or until dough gathers up on blades.

Mrs. Byrn's Chess Pie

Ingredients for 1 9-inch pie:
1¼ cups sugar
4 Tbl. softened butter
3 eggs, room temperature and lightly
  beaten
1 Tbl. cider vinegar
1 Tbl. cornmeal
1 tsp. salt
2 Tbl. milk
9-inch unbaked pie crust

Directions:
Preheat oven to 400°. In bowl of electric mixer, cream sugar and butter, until soft and fluffy. Add eggs, all at once. Continue beating, until light. Mix in remaining ingredients, except pie shell. Combine well. Pour into prepared pie crust. Reduce heat to 300°. Bake about 1 hour, or until pie is firm.

Note:
    A cherished family recipe from my grandmother, who used to pour this batter into miniature crusts; the pies were baked and frozen for unexpected guests.

Simple Pecan Pie

Ingredients for 1 9-inch pie:
1 9-inch unbaked pie shell
3 eggs
1 cup sugar
½ cup light corn syrup
6 Tbl. butter, melted
1 tsp. vanilla extract
1 cup pecans, chopped *or* pecan halves

Directions:
Preheat oven to 350°. Prepare pie crust. Set aside. In mixing bowl, beat eggs. Gradually beat in sugar, until light. Add corn syrup, butter, and vanilla extract. Fold in pecans. Pour mixture into pie crust. Bake 45-60 minutes, or until knife inserted in center comes out clean.

Note:
    Simple is best. The slow cooking time makes the most wonderful pecan pie.

Sunday Sweet Potato Pie

Ingredients for 1 9-inch pie:
1 9-inch unbaked pie shell
½ cup packed dark brown sugar
1 tsp. cinnamon
½ tsp. nutmeg
½ tsp. allspice
½ tsp. salt
1½ cups sweet potatoes, cooked and
   mashed
2 eggs
¾ cup milk
2 Tbl. butter, melted
¼ cup bourbon
sweetened whipped cream

Directions:
Prepare crust. Set aside. Preheat oven to 400°. In mixing bowl, combine sugar, cinnamon, nutmeg, allspice, and salt. Stir in potatoes. Add eggs. Beat well. Add milk, butter, and bourbon. Pour mixture into prepared pie crust. Bake 25-35 minutes, or until pie tests done. Let cool. Chill to serve. Serve with sweetened whipped cream.

Note:
   Anne Nicholson of Atlanta, to whom this recipe belongs, says pumpkin can be substituted for sweet potatoes if desired.

Chocolate Bourbon Pecan Pie

Ingredients for 1 9-inch pie:
1 9-inch unbaked pie shell
4 oz. semisweet chocolate
½ cup light brown sugar
4 eggs
½ cup light corn syrup
⅔ cup bourbon, flamed and cooled
1 Tbl. molasses
1 tsp. salt
2 cups pecan halves

Directions:
Prepare pie crust. Set aside. Preheat oven to 425°. Melt chocolate in top of double boiler over simmering water. Transfer to mixing bowl. Beat with sugar, until fluffy. Beat in eggs, 1 at a time. Stir in corn syrup, bourbon, molasses, and salt. Fold in pecans. Pour batter into pie shell. Bake 10 minutes. Lower temperature to 325°. Bake 30 minutes, or until set.

Note:
   A dark, dense, bittersweet pie. Serve with a dollop of sweetened whipped cream on top.

Black Bottom Pie

Ingredients for 1 9-inch pie:

Ingredients for crust:
14 ginger snaps
5 Tbl. butter

Ingredients for filling:
2 cups milk
4 egg yolks
3 Tbl. flour
½ cup sugar
½ oz. unsweetened chocolate
1 tsp. vanilla extract
1 Tbl. unflavored gelatin dissolved in
    ¼ cup water
4 egg whites
½ cup sugar
¼ tsp. cream of tartar
3 Tbl. bourbon
whipped cream, as garnish
grated chocolate, as garnish

Directions:
Preheat oven to 375°. Make crust: Crush ginger snaps. Melt butter. Combine. Press into bottom and sides of 9-inch pie pan. Bake 10 minutes. Set aside.

Make filling: Scald milk. Set aside. Place yolks in top of double boiler over simmering water. Add scalded milk. Stir well, to combine. Add flour and ½ cup sugar. Cook, stirring, 20 minutes, or until thick.

Remove custard from heat. Measure out 1 cup custard. Combine with chocolate and vanilla extract in a saucepan. Stir, until chocolate has melted. Cool slightly. Pour into crust. Chill until set.

To remaining custard, add gelatin dissolved in water, egg whites beaten until stiff (to which cream of tartar and ½ cup sugar have been added), and bourbon. Fold in ingredients well. Pour over chocolate layer. Chill. Whip cream. Pile on top before serving. Garnish with grated chocolate. Makes 1 9-inch pie.

Note:
Nilda Hinton of Nashville, Tennessee. The pie is pretty and easily made ahead of time.

Pecan Lemon Tart

Ingredients for 1 9-inch pie:
1 pre-baked 9-inch pie shell, cooled
¾ cup light corn syrup
6 Tbl. butter, softened
½ cup packed light brown sugar
3 eggs, lightly beaten
¼ cup lemon juice
2 Tbl. flour
2 tsp. lemon rind, grated
1¼ cups pecans, chopped
whipped cream, for topping (optional)

Directions:
Preheat oven to 375°. Combine ingredients, except pecans and whipped cream, in mixing bowl. Beat mixture until smooth. Stir in pecans. Pour filling into shell. Bake 40 minutes. Transfer to rack. Cool 20 minutes, even if filling has not set. Serve with whipped cream if desired.

Note:
Pecan pies are best not tampered with, but here lemon cuts the pie's sweetness.

Fried Apple Pies

Ingredients for 16 pies:
1 cup dried apples
water
½ cup sugar
¼ tsp. ground cinnamon
2 cups flour
3 tsp. baking powder
1 tsp. salt
¼ cup vegetable shortening
¾ cup milk
vegetable oil, for frying

Directions:
Cover apples with water in saucepan. Add sugar and cinnamon. Over medium heat, cook until very soft and moist. Mash apples. Set aside.

Make dough: Sift together flour, baking powder, and salt. Cut in shortening. Stir in milk to make soft dough. Round up dough on lightly floured board. Knead lightly. Roll out to ¼-inch thick. Cut into 2-inch round shapes. Roll round, until thin. Place spoonful of apple mixture in dough. Fold over, to make half moon. Press edges together with fork. Heat 1 inch vegetable oil in heavy skillet over medium-high heat. Fry pies in hot oil, until golden brown on both sides.

Note:
A roommate in college used to receive these in a "care" package from home.

Shirley's Lemon Meringue Pie

Ingredients for 1 9-inch pie:
1 pre-baked 9-inch pie shell
6 Tbl. cornstarch
1 cup sugar
1½ cups water
2 egg yolks, beaten
pinch salt
3 Tbl. butter
5 Tbl. lemon juice
rind of 2 lemons, grated

Ingredients for meringue:
3 egg whites
7 Tbl. superfine sugar
pinch salt

Directions:
Preheat oven to 425°. In saucepan, heat cornstarch, sugar, and water, stirring until thick, over medium heat. Remove from heat. Add egg yolks. Return pan to heat. Bring to boil, stirring constantly. Simmer a few minutes. Add salt, butter, lemon juice, and lemon rind. Mix well. Pour into prepared crust.

Beat egg whites, until soft peaks form and whites just barely slip in the bowl. Add sugar. Beat whites until they no longer slip. Add tiny bit of salt.

Pile meringue on hot filling. Be sure to spread out to edges, to seal in filling. Bake 4½ minutes, or until meringue is light brown.

Note:
Shirley Corriher of Atlanta says the tricks to a perfect lemon meringue pie are: (1) Do not scramble your egg yolks when adding to a hot base for filling, and (2) Do not overbeat your whites for meringue.

🙠 Mrs. Byrn's Chess Pie (page 164)

Mrs. Foote's Sugar Cookies (page 174)

Shaker Lemon Pie

Ingredients for 1 9-inch pie:
2 large, thin-skinned lemons
2 cups sugar
4 eggs, well beaten
1 double recipe 9-inch unbaked pie crust

Directions:
Slice lemons (including rind) as thinly as paper. Remove seeds from slices. Combine slices with sugar. Let stand 2 hours or longer, stirring occasionally. (Make pie crust during this time.)

Preheat oven to 450°. Add beaten eggs to lemon mixture. Mix well. Turn into 9-inch pie shell. Arrange lemon slices evenly. Cover with top crust. Cut several slits near center. Bake at 450° 15 minutes. Reduce heat to 375°. Bake 20 minutes longer, or until knife inserted near edge of pie comes out clean. Cool before serving.

Note:
From Mildred Finnell of East Point, Georgia, winner of Atlanta pie baking contest in 1978.

Caramel Brownies

Ingredients for 2½ dozen brownies:
1 cup butter
4 oz. unsweetened chocolate
4 eggs
2 cups sugar
1 cup flour
1 tsp. vanilla extract
1 tsp. salt
½ cup nuts, chopped (optional)
1 14-oz. bag caramels
scant ⅓ cup evaporated milk

Directions:
Preheat oven to 350°. Melt together butter and chocolate in small saucepan. Let cool. Beat eggs and sugar in large mixing bowl. Add cooled chocolate mixture. Add flour, vanilla extract, and salt. Stir in nuts, if desired. Pour half mixture into greased, 13-by-9-inch baking pan. Bake 15 minutes. Meanwhile, heat caramels and milk over low heat, stirring, until caramels are melted. Spread caramel mixture over first layer of baked brownie. Top with remaining half of brownie batter. Return to oven. Bake 30 minutes. Cool. Cut into squares.

Note:
This recipe comes from Diane Camara of Marietta, Georgia, who entered it in *The Atlanta Journal-Constitution* Food Guide's brownie contest in the fall of 1983 and won first place. More than 650 recipes from readers were submitted. It is gooey and a hit with children.

Crème De Menthe Brownies

Ingredients for 2 dozen brownies:
½ cup butter
1 cup sugar
4 eggs, beaten
1 cup flour
½ tsp. salt
1 16-oz. can chocolate syrup
1 tsp. vanilla extract
2 cups confectioners' sugar
½ cup butter
2 Tbl. crème de menthe
1 cup chocolate chips
6 Tbl. butter

Directions:
Preheat oven to 350°. Cream ½ cup butter and sugar together. Add eggs. Beat well. Gradually fold in flour, then salt, chocolate syrup, and vanilla extract. Pour batter into greased, 13-by-9-inch pan. Bake 20-25 minutes.

When cake is cool, mix together confectioners' sugar, ½ cup butter, and crème de menthe. Spread over cake.

Melt chocolate chips and 6 Tbl. butter in small saucepan. Let cool until it will spread easily. Spread over brownies. Chill 2 hours. Cut into squares.

Blond Brownies

Ingredients for 1 9-inch square pan:
1 cup sifted flour
½ tsp. baking powder
⅛ tsp. baking soda
½ tsp. salt
½ cup walnuts, chopped *or* pecans, chopped
⅓ cup butter
1 cup firmly packed brown sugar
1 egg, lightly beaten
1 tsp. vanilla extract
½ cup semisweet chocolate morsels

Directions:
Preheat oven to 350°. In medium mixing bowl, combine flour, baking powder, soda, and salt. Add nuts. Toss to combine. In small saucepan, melt butter. Mix in brown sugar. Pour butter-sugar mixture into large mixing bowl. Allow to cool. Stir in egg and vanilla extract. Slowly add dry ingredients, combining well. Spread batter into greased, 9-inch square pan. Sprinkle morsels over top. Bake 20-25 minutes. Makes about 16 squares.

Note:
Let cool in pan before cutting into squares.

Mother's Pan Brownies

Ingredients for 2½ dozen brownies:
1 cup butter, softened
2 cups sugar
4 eggs
8 Tbl. cocoa
1 cup sifted flour
¼ tsp. salt
¼ tsp. baking powder
1 cup pecans, chopped
1 tsp. vanilla extract

Directions:
Preheat oven to 350°. Cream butter with sugar in mixing bowl. Add eggs, 1 at a time, beating after each addition. Add cocoa. Blend well. Add flour, salt, and baking powder. Fold in nuts and vanilla extract. Mix to incorporate all ingredients. Pour into greased, 13-by-9-inch baking pan. Bake 28-32 minutes, or until top is crusty and brownies begin to pull away from sides of pan. Cool. Cut into squares.

Note:
One of my favorite recipes from the newspaper contest, this brownie formula was a runner-up, and is originally from the mother of Beverly Brooks of Morrow, Georgia.

Butterscotch Brownies

Ingredients for 2½ dozen brownies:
1 cup butter
1 lb. light brown sugar
2 eggs
2 cups sifted flour
1 tsp. baking powder
1 tsp. vanilla extract
2 cups pecans, coarsely chopped

Directions: Preheat oven to 375°. Melt butter in 13-by-9-inch pan. Put sugar in large mixing bowl. Pour melted butter over. Cream butter and sugar. Beat in eggs. Mix in remaining ingredients. Pour back into already-buttered pan. Bake 25-30 minutes, or until brownies begin to pull away from sides of pan. When cool, cut into squares or bars.

Note:
    From Mrs. Ted Debreceni of Atlanta who entered this classic recipe in the Food Guide's brownie contest.

Celestial Brownies

Ingredients for 1 8-inch square pan:
½ cup butter
8 oz. semisweet chocolate
2 eggs, room temperature
¾ cup sugar
1 tsp. vanilla extract
¼ cup flour
1 cup pecans, chopped
confectioners' sugar

Directions:
Preheat oven to 350°. Grease 8-inch square baking pan. Set aside. Melt butter and chocolate in heavy-bottomed pan. Set aside. Beat eggs in medium mixer bowl at high speed 1 minute. Gradually add sugar, beating until mixture is pale yellow and fluffy, about 4 minutes. Reduce mixer speed. Add chocolate mixture and vanilla extract to egg mixture, until blended. Add flour until well absorbed. Stir in nuts. Spoon batter into prepared pan. Bake about 30 minutes, or until cake tests done. Place on wire rack and cool. Cut into squares. Dust with powdered sugar. Makes 16 squares.

Coffee Liqueur Brownies

Ingredients for 1 9-inch square pan:
⅔ cup butter
3 oz. unsweetened chocolate
3 eggs, room temperature
2 cups sugar
¼ cup coffee liqueur
1½ cups sifted flour
½ tsp. baking powder
½ tsp. salt
¾ cup pecans, chopped
1 Tbl. coffee liqueur

Directions:
Preheat oven to 350°. In small saucepan, melt butter and chocolate over very low heat, watching so chocolate doesn't burn. Set aside. In medium mixing bowl, beat eggs and sugar until light and fluffy. Stir in cooled chocolate mixture and ¼ cup coffee liqueur. Mix well. Add flour, baking powder, and salt. Combine. Stir in nuts. Turn batter into greased, 9-inch square pan lined with greased foil or waxed paper. Bake 30 minutes, or until center springs back when lightly touched. Don't overbake. Remove from oven. Cool. Spread top with 1 Tbl. coffee liqueur. Makes about 16 large brownies.

Note:
    No better dessert than this brownie topped with vanilla ice cream.

Creamy Chocolate Fudge

Ingredients for 1¾ lbs.:
3 cups semisweet chocolate bits
1 14-oz. can sweetened condensed milk
dash salt
1 tsp. vanilla extract
½ cup pecans, chopped

Directions:
In top of double boiler, melt chocolate over boiling water, stirring. Remove from heat. Add remaining ingredients. Stir with wooden spoon, until smooth. Spread mixture into 8-inch square baking pan which has been lined with waxed paper. Chill 2 hours, or until firm. Turn onto cutting board. Peel off paper. Cut into squares.

Variations:
    Instead of adding vanilla extract, substitute an orange or coffee liqueur.

Purcell's Afternoon Teas

Ingredients for 3 dozen cookies:
½ cup butter
½ cup sugar
2 egg yolks, slightly beaten
1½ cups flour
pecan halves *or* candied cherry halves

Directions:
Preheat oven to 350°. In mixing bowl, cream butter and sugar, until light. Add egg yolks. Blend well. Gradually beat in flour. Dough will be stiff. With hands, form dough into 1-inch rounds. Place on greased baking sheets. Press pecan half into each ball. Bake about 10 minutes, or until cookies are golden, but not brown. Store in cookie jar.

Note:
   A favorite recipe of my grandmother, Eliza Carr. Make with cherries during Christmas for a festive look.

Mrs. Foote's Sugar Cookies

Ingredients for 4 to 5 dozen cookies:
1½ cups sugar
1 cup vegetable shortening
3 eggs
1 tsp. baking soda
1 tsp. baking powder
4½-5 cups sifted flour
4 Tbl. milk
2 tsp. vanilla extract

Directions:
In mixing bowl, cream sugar and shortening, until light. Add eggs, 1 at a time, beating well after each addition. In separate bowl, combine baking soda, baking powder, and flour. Add to creamed mixture alternately with milk. After all dry ingredients are incorporated, mix in vanilla extract. Chill dough about 1 hour. Preheat oven to 350°. Roll out to desired thickness. Cut into shapes. Bake on ungreased cookie sheets 10-15 minutes, or until browned around edges.

Note:
   These can be decorated for Christmas by children.

Rich Chocolate Chip Cookies

Ingredients for 4 dozen cookies:
½ cup plus 2 Tbl. butter, softened
¼ cup sugar
½ cup packed light brown sugar
1 egg
1 tsp. vanilla extract
⅛ tsp. almond extract
1 cup flour
½ tsp. baking soda
¼ tsp. salt
6 oz. semisweet chocolate, broken into bits
1 cup walnuts, coarsely chopped

Directions:
In mixing bowl, cream butter with sugars, until light. Beat in egg and vanilla and almond extracts. In separate bowl, combine flour, soda, and salt. Gradually add to creamed mixture. Fold in chocolate and nuts. Refrigerate dough 30 minutes. Preheat oven to 350°. Onto ungreased cookie sheets, drop dough by spoonfuls. Bake 12-15 minutes.

Note:
You can substitute pecans or macadamia nuts for the walnuts or add half nuts, half raisins.

Homemade Banana Pudding

Ingredients for 4 to 6 servings:
⅓ cup flour
⅔ cup sugar
2 cups milk
2 egg yolks, lightly beaten
½ tsp. vanilla extract
vanilla wafers
3-4 bananas, sliced
3 egg whites
¼ tsp. cream of tartar
¼ cup sugar

Directions:
Preheat oven to 350°. Combine flour and sugar in 2-quart saucepan. Mix well. Stir in milk, egg yolks, and vanilla extract. Cook over medium heat, stirring, until mixture thickens. Cover bottom of greased, 8-inch, round baking dish with layer of vanilla wafers. Top with ½ banana slices and ½ pudding. Repeat layers, ending with pudding.

Beat egg whites until soft peaks form. Add cream of tartar and then gradually sugar, continuing to beat until whites hold a peak, but are not dry. Spread meringue over pudding, sealing edges of baking dish. Bake 10-12 minutes, or until meringue is golden.

Luscious Chocolate Fondue

Ingredients for 1½ cups:
8 oz. dark, sweetened chocolate
⅔ cup heavy cream
6 Tbl. kirsch
1 tsp. cinnamon
1 tsp. nutmeg
fresh peaches and whole strawberries, to
   dip

Directions:
Melt chocolate in double boiler over simmering water. Add remaining ingredients except fruit. Stir until smooth. Place in fondue pot over low flame. Serve with slices of fresh peaches and whole strawberries to dip.

Roxanna's Chocolate Mousse

Ingredients for 4 servings:
⅔ cup semisweet chocolate morsels
1 Tbl. butter, room temperature
4 tsp. grand Marnier
3 egg whites
2 tsp. sugar
4 navel oranges, cut into sections

Directions:
Melt chocolate in double boiler over hot water. Stir in butter and grand Marnier. Remove pan from heat. Leave chocolate mixture sitting over the hot water. (If it gets too cold, the mousse will be lumpy; if too hot, the mixture will deflate egg whites.)

Place egg white beater in the work bowl of food processor. If processor hasn't such attachment, beat egg whites with electric mixer or by hand, until soft peaks form. Add sugar. Whip until stiff. Fold egg white mixture into chocolate mixture. Place ½ of orange sections in bottoms of 4 wine glasses. Top with ½ mousse. Add remaining orange sections. Top with more mousse. Chill at least 3 hours.

Note:
From Roxanna Young, an Atlantan with Robot Coupe.

Rose's Chocolate Mousse

Ingredients for 6 servings:
3 egg yolks
1½ Tbl. water
2 Tbl. cognac
4 oz. Tobler extra bittersweet chocolate,
   melted
1 cup heavy cream
pinch salt
3 egg whites
1 Tbl. superfine sugar

Directions:
In heavy saucepan over low heat, whisk yolks and water constantly, until yolks start to thicken. Whisk in cognac. Continue whisking, until mixture starts to thicken to the consistency of hollandaise sauce. Remove from heat. Fold in melted chocolate. Remove to mixing bowl. In small bowl, beat cream just until stiff peaks form. Fold cream into chocolate mixture. Add pinch of salt to egg whites. Beat to soft peaks. Beat in sugar, until stiff peaks form. Fold small amount of whites into chocolate mixture, to lighten. Then fold in remaining whites. Spoon into serving bowl. Chill.

Note:
   Rose Levy Beranbaum of New York City is one of our best dessert creators. This is one of her specialties.

Lemon Bars

Ingredients for 1 9-inch square pan:
¼ cup confectioners' sugar
½ cup butter, softened
1 cup flour
pinch salt
2 eggs
1 cup sugar
2 Tbl. fresh lemon juice
rind of 1 lemon, grated
2 Tbl. flour

Directions:
Preheat oven to 350°. Cream confectioners' sugar with butter, until fluffy. Add 1 cup flour and salt. Mix well. Press mixture into bottom of greased 9-inch square pan. Bake 15 minutes. In mixing bowl, beat eggs. Add sugar, lemon juice, lemon rind, and 2 Tbl. flour. Pour batter over baked crust. Bake 20 minutes more. Makes 16 bars.

Poppy Seed Torte

Ingredients for crust:
1 cup flour
¼ cup packed light brown sugar
½ cup unsalted butter
½ cup walnuts, chopped

Ingredients for filling:
1 cup sugar
2 Tbl. cornstarch
¼ tsp. salt
1½ cups milk
5 egg yolks
¼ cup poppy seeds
1½ envelopes plain gelatin dissolved in
    1½ cups cold water
5 egg whites
½ tsp. cream of tartar
½ cup sugar
½ tsp. vanilla extract
whipped cream, as garnish

Directions:
Preheat oven to 350°. Make crust: Combine flour and sugar in mixing bowl. Cut in butter with 2 sharp knives, as if making biscuits. Fold in nuts. Mix well. Pat into bottom of greased 13-by-9-inch pan. Bake 12-15 minutes.

Meanwhile, make filling: Combine 1 cup sugar, cornstarch, salt, milk, and egg yolks in top of double boiler over simmering water. Cook, stirring, about 5 minutes. Add poppy seeds and dissolved gelatin. Cook until thick, stirring, 15 minutes more.

Beat egg whites along with cream of tartar, ½ cup sugar, and vanilla extract, until very stiff. Fold this meringue into slightly cooled custard. Pour over crust. Cover. Chill at least 2 hours before serrving. Cut into squares. Serve with whipped cream on top.

Note:
From Evelyn Roughton of The Crown Restaurant in the Antique Mall in Indianola, Mississippi.

Peach Ice Cream

Ingredients for 1 gallon:
6 cups fresh peaches, mashed
1 cup sugar
5 eggs
2 cups sugar
¼ tsp. salt
1 tsp. vanilla extract
½ cup milk
1 cup heavy cream, whipped
1 cup half-and-half
about 1 quart milk

Directions:
Combine peaches with 1 cup sugar. Mix well. Set aside. Beat eggs with electric mixer at medium speed, until frothy. Gradually add 2 cups sugar to eggs. Beat until thick. Add salt, vanilla extract, and ½ cup milk. Beat, until sugar has dissolved. Stir in whipped cream, half-and-half, and peach mixture. Pour mixture into freezer container of 1-gallon ice cream maker. Add enough milk to fill can ⅔ full. Freeze according to manufacturer's instructions. Let ripen 1 hour.

Peach Cobbler

Ingredients for 6 servings:
4 cups fresh peaches, peeled and sliced
1 cup sugar
½ cup butter
1½ cups flour
¾ tsp. salt
½ cup vegetable shortening
¼ cup plus 1 Tbl. cold water

Directions:
Preheat oven to 350°. Combine peaches, sugar, and butter in medium saucepan. Bring to boil. Reduce heat. Simmer, until peaches are tender and mixture thickens, about 20 minutes. Pour mixture into buttered 10-by-6-by-2-inch baking dish. Set aside. In mixing bowl, combine flour and salt. Cut in shortening with 2 knives, until mixture resembles coarse crumbs. Sprinkle water over flour mixture until ingredients are moistened. Shape pastry into ball. Roll out to ⅛-inch thickness on lightly floured board. Cut into 1-inch strips. Arrange ½ strips in lattice design over peaches. Bake 35 minutes. Remove from oven. Gently press remaining strips over baked strips in lattice pattern. Press pastry into peach mixture. Return to oven. Bake another 40 minutes.

Year 'Round Apple Cobbler

Ingredients for 6 to 8 servings:
8 cups tart baking apples, peeled and
   sliced
¾ cup packed light brown sugar
1 tsp. cinnamon
1 tsp. nutmeg
⅓ cup sweet white wine
1 cup flour
2 tsp. baking powder
1 Tbl. sugar
dash salt
¼ cup butter
⅓ cup milk
1 egg, beaten
sugar

Directions:
In mixing bowl, toss apples with brown sugar
and spices. Arrange in 9-inch square or
round baking dish. Pour wine over. Preheat
oven to 400° and set apples in oven about 10
minutes while making topping. In mixing
bowl, combine flour, baking powder, sugar,
and salt. Cut in butter with 2 knives, until
mixture resembles coarse meal. Stir in milk
and egg, just until ingredients are moistened. Remove apples from oven; drop
batter by spoonfuls over apples. Sprinkle
with additional sugar. Return to oven. Bake
35-45 minutes or until apples are tender and
topping is golden brown. Serve warm with
ice cream.

Note:
   Any tart apple will work in this recipe,
and during the summer months, you can
always use Granny Smith apples.

Blueberry Buckle

Ingredients for 6 to 8 servings:
¼ cup butter, softened
¾ cup sugar
1 egg
½ cup milk
2 cups sifted cake flour
2 tsp. baking powder
½ tsp. salt
2 cups fresh blueberries

Ingredients for topping:
¼ cup butter, softened
½ cup brown sugar
⅓ cup sifted flour
½ tsp. cinnamon
ice cream *or* whipped cream, to serve

Directions:
Preheat oven to 350°. Cream butter and sugar, until light. In separate bowl, beat egg. Add milk. Sift flour, baking powder, and salt. Add to creamed mixture, along with milk and egg mixture. Fold in blueberries. Spread batter in greased and floured 9-inch, square pan.

Making topping: Cream butter with brown sugar and flour. Add cinnamon. Sprinkle over batter in pan. Bake 30-35 minutes. Serve warm with ice cream or whipped cream.

Crescent Cookies

Ingredients for 6 dozen cookies:
1 cup unsalted butter, softened
2 tsp. vanilla extract
8 Tbl. confectioners' sugar
2 cups flour
2 cups pecans, chopped
confectioners' sugar

Directions:
Preheat oven to 275°. Cream butter and vanilla extract. Add sugar. Cream well. Add flour to combine. Mix in nuts with wooden spoon. Dough will be stiff. Pinch off pieces of dough. Shape into crescents. Place on ungreased baking sheets. Bake about 30 minutes, or until just light brown. Sprinkle with or roll in confectioners' sugar while warm.

Pecan Brittle

Ingredients for 1¼ lbs.:
2 cups sugar
3 cups pecans, coarsely chopped
¾ cup white corn syrup
¼ cup water
3 tsp. baking soda

Directions:
Combine sugar, pecans, corn syrup, and water in heavy-bottomed skillet. Cook over medium heat, stirring, until candy thermometer registers 290°. Stir in soda quickly. Mixture will foam up. Pour onto greased baking sheet. Spread out with spatula. Allow to cool well, about 2 hours. Break into pieces. Store in airtight container.

Note:
    An alternative to peanut brittle. Makes a nice gift.

Rum Balls

Ingredients for 3 dozen balls:
1 cup butter, softened
1½ lbs. confectioners' sugar
½ cup light rum
1 10-inch round angel food cake
1 lb. pecans, finely ground

Directions:
In mixing bowl, cream butter and sugar. Add rum, until consistency to spread. Cut cake into 1½-inch blocks. Spread butter-rum mixture on cake on all sides. Roll in nuts.

Shortbread

Ingredients for 2 dozen cookies:
2 cups butter, softened
4 cups flour
1¼ cups confectioners' sugar
1 tsp. baking powder
¼ tsp. salt

Directions:
Preheat oven to 325°. In large mixing bowl, cut butter into flour with 2 knives, as if making biscuits. With hands, work in confectioners' sugar, baking powder, and salt. Knead, until well mixed. Pat dough into 2 9-inch round cake pans. With fork, prick dough over top. Bake 45 minutes, or until golden. While warm, cut each pan into 12 wedges. Cool in pans on wire racks. Remove from pans. Place in airtight tins. Perfect for gift-giving.

Sauces & Spreads

Three Cherished Gravies

Good Southern gravies, like bad tidings, come in threes. Milk, red-eye, and tomato gravies are as dear to the South as a bolognese sauce is to Italy or beurre blanc is to France.

Call them fattening if you like, but folks down South have been soaking biscuits in tomato gravy and pouring red-eye gravy over grits and milk gravy over potatoes and rice for some time.

Milk gravy, or cream gravy when cream is substituted for milk, is just a simple white sauce formula. To drippings in a skillet, you add an equal amount of flour to thicken, stir over medium-low heat, and then gradually whisk in warmed milk. Season to taste with salt and pepper. It's the browned bits that cling to the bottom of the skillet and are stirred into the sauce as it cooks which make milk gravy distinctive.

Tomato gravy is nothing more than canned stewed tomatoes which are added to a skillet after browning 2 Tbl. flour in 3 Tbl. bacon drippings and diced onion. Season well with salt and pepper. This goes especially well with black-eyed peas and biscuits.

Red-eye gravy, however, will stir up debate. Some people add water to the drippings after frying country ham slices. Others prefer to add ½ cup black coffee to make a reddish brown pungent sauce. It just depends on who taught you how to make red-eye gravy.

Once the basic techniques are mastered, there's room only for improvement with these 3 Southern gravies.

Food Processor Hollandaise Sauce

Ingredients for 1½ cups:
4 egg yolks, room temperature
juice of 3 lemons
1 cup butter, melted and still hot
pinch salt
pinch cayenne pepper

Directions:
Place yolks and lemon juice in bowl of food processor fitted with steel blade. With motor running, drizzle in hot butter. If sauce doesn't thicken in processor, transfer to saucepan. Heat carefully over low heat with constant whisking, until thick. Remove from heat. Continue to whisk. Season with salt and cayenne pepper.

Note:
Sometimes this sauce doesn't thicken. Just heat over a low flame while whisking, and it should turn out thick and rich. Serve over steamed asparagus, broccoli, or Eggs Benedict.

Food Processor Mayonnaise

Ingredients for 1 cup:
1 egg
1 Tbl. lemon juice
1 tsp. Dijon-style mustard *or* dry mustard
1 tsp. salt
1 cup vegetable oil

Directions:
Place all ingredients, except vegetable oil, in bowl of food processor fitted with steel blade. With motor running, gradually dribble in oil, until mixture is thick.

Note:
Should your mayonnaise fail, remove mixture from food processor bowl, clean bowl well, add a blob of commercial mayonnaise to bowl, and gradually add back your attempt at a mayonnaise. A new emulsion will form.

ody's Pesto Sauce

Ingredients for 2 cups:
1 cup fresh basil
½ cup fresh parsley, chopped
½ cup Parmesan cheese, grated
¼ cup pine nuts
2 cloves garlic
¼ tsp. salt
½ cup olive oil

Directions:
In blender container or bowl of food processor, place basil, parsley, Parmesan cheese, pine nuts, garlic, and salt. Blend or process with steel blade, until it forms paste. With motor running, gradually add oil, until sauce is consistency of soft butter. Serve over hot pasta or with sliced fresh tomatoes.

Note:
My sister-in-law's recipe is served most often with pasta, but pesto is versatile and able to accompany scrambled eggs or grilled chicken or fish if need be.

Mustard Vinaigrette

Ingredients for ½ cup:
2 Tbl. Dijon-style mustard
2 Tbl. red wine vinegar
salt, to taste
black pepper, freshly ground, to taste
1 clove garlic, crushed
½ cup olive oil

Directions:
Place mustard in small bowl with vinegar, salt, pepper, and garlic. Whisk until smooth. Gradually add oil, whisking until smooth and thick.

Note:
This simple dressing should be tossed with crisp salad greens to accompany a pizza, lasagna, or roasted chicken. It can be made quickly in a blender or food processor.

Last-Minute Spaghetti Sauce

Ingredients for 4 servings:
2 Tbl. olive oil
1 cup onion, minced
3 cloves garlic, minced
1 lb. lean ground beef
salt, to taste
black pepper, to taste
3 cups canned Italian tomatoes, drained
3 Tbl. tomato paste
¾ cup dry red wine
¼ tsp. red pepper flakes
1 Tbl. sugar
1 tsp. dried basil, crumbled
½ tsp. dried oregano, crumbled
¼ tsp. dried rosemary, crumbled
hot pasta, to serve

Directions:
Heat oil in skillet. Add onion and garlic. Cook, stirring, over medium-low heat until soft. Add meat. Cook until meat loses its raw color. Salt and pepper to taste. Blend tomatoes and tomato paste in food processor or blender. Add tomato mixture to meat, along with wine, red pepper flakes, sugar, basil, oregano, and rosemary. Cook, uncovered, over moderately low heat 30-45 minutes. Serve over hot pasta.

Creamy Horseradish Sauce

Ingredients for 1⅓ cups:
1 cup sour cream
⅓ cup prepared horseradish
1 tsp. red wine vinegar
½ tsp. Dijon-style mustard

Directions:
In medium-sized bowl, whisk together sour cream and horseradish. Stir in vinegar and mustard. Blend well. Chill, covered. Serve with smoked fish or cold, sliced beef.

Note:
This sauce is delicious with smoked trout or mullet.

Sesame Seed Butter

Ingredients for enough sauce for 6
   servings of beans:
½ cup butter
2 Tbl. sesame seeds
juice of 1 lemon
salt, to taste

Directions:
Brown butter in small skillet. Add sesame
seeds. Allow seeds to brown and butter to
foam. Squeeze juice of lemon into foaming
butter. Stir. Serve over hot, drained green
beans. Toss well to cover. Salt if needed.

Note:
   From The Crown Restaurant in Indianola, Mississippi.

Pecan-Honey Butter

Ingredients for 2 cups:
¼ cup honey
1 cup butter, softened
½ cup pecans, chopped

Directions:
Slowly beat honey into butter, until well
blended. Stir in pecans. Pack into crock or
gift container, if desired. Refrigerate. Bring
to room temperature before serving on
biscuits, rolls, and sweet breads.

Brandy Hard Sauce

Ingredients for 1½ cups:
½ cup butter, softened
1½ cups confectioners' sugar
½ tsp. vanilla extract
1 Tbl. brandy
⅛ tsp. nutmeg

Directions:
Cream butter in small mixing bowl. Gradually add sugar. Beat well. Add vanilla extract, brandy, and nutmeg. Beat well. Chill. Serve with fruitcake or steamed plum pudding.

Note:
Bring to room temperature just before serving.

Lemon Mayonnaise

Ingredients for 1¼ cups:
2 egg yolks
2 Tbl. lemon juice, freshly squeezed
1 heaping tsp. dry mustard
dash cayenne pepper
dash salt
1 cup vegetable oil *or* olive oil

Directions:
In electric blender or food processor, blend all ingredients, except oil. With machine still running slowly, add oil in steady stream just until the mixture thickens, about 1 minute.

Note:
Easy to make. This is delicious in potato salads or spread on ham sandwiches with sliced ripe tomatoes.

Herb Butter

Ingredients for 1 cup:
1 Tbl. fresh herbs, finely chopped (e.g. basil, oregano, thyme, tarragon, *or* rosemary)
1 Tbl. fresh parsley, minced
1 Tbl. fresh chives, minced
1 cup soft butter

Directions:
Chop herbs, parsley, and chives until very fine with scissors or in the food processor. Mash butter until soft. Stir in herbs. Cover. Chill until ready to use.

Note:
Herb butters are made from any variation of fresh herbs, which are plentiful in the summer and available at farmers' markets during the winter months. Use on steamed vegetables, grilled meats and seafoods, and homemade breads. This is also tasty for frying eggs or on baked potatoes. Take care when heating herb butter, for the fresh herbs burn easily.

Applesauce

Ingredients for 4 servings:
1 lb. cooking apples, peeled, cored, and quartered
cold water
2 tsp. lemon rind, grated
1 Tbl. water
2 tsp. sugar
2 tsp. butter

Directions:
Place apple quarters in bowl of cold water to retain color while preparing. Drain. Turn into saucepan with lemon rind. Add 1 Tbl. water. Bring to boil. Cover. Cook until apples are soft and pulpy, about 15-20 minutes. Beat well. Add sugar and butter.

Note:
This recipe can be varied by adding a dash of cinnamon or nutmeg and by using brown sugar instead of granulated.

Curry Dressing

Ingredients for ¾ cup:
6 Tbl. olive oil
2 Tbl. white wine vinegar
2 Tbl. orange juice
1 Tbl. curry powder
1 Tbl. fresh lemon *or* lime juice
salt, to taste
pepper, to taste

Directions:
In screw-top jar, combine all ingredients. Shake well to blend. Pour over Mango-Orange Salad.

Basil-Pecan Vinaigrette

Ingredients for 1 cup:
½ cup fresh basil, finely chopped
¼ cup fresh lemon juice
¼ cup olive oil
¼ cup vegetable oil
½ tsp. salt
⅓ cup pecans, chopped

Directions:
Combine basil and lemon juice in mixing bowl. Whisk in oils. Season with salt, to taste. Stir in pecans. Serve over sliced ripe tomatoes.

Tempura Batter

Ingredients for 4 servings as an appetizer:
1 egg yolk
2 cups ice water
⅛ tsp. baking soda
1⅔ cups flour
oil, for deep frying
crisp, cleaned, uncooked vegetables (e.g., button mushrooms, diagonally sliced carrots, sliced green beans, strips of sweet potato)

Directions:
Combine egg yolk, ice water, soda, and flour in mixing bowl. Stir well, but batter will be rather lumpy at first. Try to work out most of the lumps. Heat oil to 375°. Dip vegetables into batter. Drop into hot oil. Fry until light brown on all sides. If you desire to toss in a few shrimp with your vegetables, coat them with flour before dunking in batter.

Poppy Seed Dressing

Ingredients for 2 cups:
2 Tbl. prepared mustard
1 cup vegetable oil
⅓ cup red wine vinegar
⅓ cup sugar *or* honey
⅓ medium-sized sweet onion (preferably Vidalia onion), coarsely chopped
2 Tbl. poppy seeds

Directions:
Mix mustard, oil, vinegar, and sugar in food processor or blender container. Add onion and poppy seeds. Blend just until mixed. Serve over fresh fruit salads. This improves after storing in refrigerator for a few days.

Note:
    Unlike many other recipes for poppy seed dressing, this version is not too sweet. It contains less sugar, which I find accents the fresh sweetness of the fruit in the salad.

Bebe's Never-Fail Chocolate Icing

Ingredients:
2 cups sugar
½ cup cocoa
½ cup milk
½ cup butter
1 tsp. vanilla extract
dash salt

Directions:
Mix sugar, cocoa, milk, and butter in heavy-bottomed saucepan or top of double boiler. Bring to boil, stirring. Boil hard 1½ minutes. Cool. Add vanilla extract and salt. Beat with wooden spoon until desired consistency. While warm, spread over favorite chocolate 2-layer cake or recipe of brownies. Don't wait too long, or icing will set.

Homemade Pimiento Cheese Spread

Ingredients for 1½ cups:
½ lb. extra-sharp Cheddar cheese, shredded
1 4-oz. jar pimientos, chopped, liquid reserved
1 tsp. dry mustard
1 Tbl. liquid reserved from pimientos
mayonnaise, to moisten

Directions:
Combine cheese with pimientos, mustard, and liquid. Add enough mayonnaise to make consistency spreadable. Cover. Chill. This keeps for several days.

Cucumber Sauce

Ingredients for 1 cup:
½ cup mayonnaise
½ cup cucumber, peeled, seeded, and
  shredded
1 tsp. lemon peel, grated
2 tsp. fresh lemon juice
¼ tsp. dried dill weed *or* 1 tsp. fresh dill,
  minced
salt, to taste
pepper, to taste

Directions:
In small mixing bowl, combine all ingredients, except salt and pepper. Season with salt and pepper. Serve with fried or poached fish.

Primavera Dressing

Ingredients for 2½ cups:
¾ cup olive oil
¾ cup vegetable oil
1 cup red wine vinegar
1 tsp. dried oregano
2 garlic cloves, minced
2 tsp. sugar
¼ cup fresh basil, chopped
½ tsp. salt
½ tsp. black pepper
2 Tbl. onion, chopped
2 Tbl. Parmesan cheese, grated

Directions:
Place all ingredients in container of blender or food processor. Mix until smooth. Pour over Pasta Primavera Salad.

Fresh Tomato Sauce

Ingredients for 2½ cups:
5 medium-sized tomatoes, peeled
½ cup onion, chopped
2 Tbl. butter
2 cloves garlic, minced
1 Tbl. parsley, chopped
½ tsp. salt
¼ tsp. thyme *or* basil
⅛ tsp. black pepper, coarsely ground

Directions:
Chop tomatoes, removing seeds. Sauté onion in butter. Stir in tomatoes, garlic, parsley, salt, thyme, and pepper. Purée mixture in food processor or blender. Serve over spoonbread, pasta, and fresh vegetables.

Chris' Barbecue Sauce

Ingredients for enough sauce to liberally coat parts of 1 broiler-fryer chicken:
12 oz. warm beer
1½ cups ketchup
½ cup brown sugar (dark *or* light)
¼ cup red wine vinegar
2 tsp. Dijon-style mustard
1 tsp. dry mustard
1 tsp. red pepper flakes
1 tsp. dried basil
8 dashes Worcestershire sauce

Directions:
Combine all ingredients in heavy-bottomed saucepan with lid. Bring to boil. Reduce heat. Simmer, covered, about 30 minutes, so that ingredients will have time to mingle. Turn off heat. About 10 minutes before ready to use sauce, simmer uncovered, so sauce will thicken a bit.

Note:
Since my husband Chris never makes a sauce the same way twice, it was tough getting this formula from him. Feel free to substitute or omit ingredients to your liking. Best over chicken and ribs. But then, only Texans barbecue beef anyway.

Homemade Chocolate Sauce

Ingredients for 3 cups:
2 cups sugar
5 level Tbl. flour
8 Tbl. cocoa
dash salt
2 cups milk
2 Tbl. butter
2 tsp. vanilla extract

Directions:
Sift together sugar, flour, cocoa, and salt. Place in top of double boiler. Add milk, butter, and vanilla extract. Cook over low heat, stirring constantly, until mixture is thickened. Adjust seasoning, if desired. Serve atop homemade ice cream or toasted pound cake.

Note:
From Martha Ellis, Nashville, Tennessee.

Mustard Spread

Ingredients for 2¼ cups:
1 cup butter, softened
2 Tbl. poppy seeds
1 large onion, coarsely chopped
5 tsp. prepared mustard (Dijon is nice)

Directions:
Blend all ingredients in blender or process in food processor until smooth. Refrigerate at least 24 hours.

Spread on split biscuits with ham or put mix in a French roll split lengthwise. Add ham and cheese and take on a picnic.

Pickled Hot Peppers

Ingredients for 8 pints:
1½ cups salt
1 gallon hot water
4 quarts banana peppers *or* any other hot peppers, slit up sides
10 cups vinegar
2 cups water
¼ cup sugar
2 Tbl. prepared horseradish
2 cloves garlic, peeled

Directions:
Dissolve salt in gallon of hot water. Pour over peppers in glass or pottery bowl. Let stand 12-18 hours in cool place. Rinse. Drain. Set aside. Combine remaining ingredients in large saucepan. Bring to boil. Simmer 15 minutes. Remove garlic. Pack peppers into pint jars. Bring liquid back to boil. Pour into jars. Seal. Process in boiling water bath 10 minutes.

Note:
From Pat Bruschini of the Cobb County (Georgia) Extension Service.

Pickled Green Beans

Ingredients for 4 pints:
2 lbs. green beans, washed and broken into 2-inch pieces
1 tsp. cayenne pepper
4 heads fresh dill *or* 4 tsp. dill seed
4 cloves garlic
2½ cups water
2½ cups white vinegar
¼ cup salt

Directions:
Wash, drain, and cut beans. Pack lengthwise into 4 1-pint jars with ½-inch head space. To each pint, add ¼ tsp. cayenne pepper, 1 head fresh dill and 1 clove garlic. Combine water, vinegar, and salt in small saucepan. Bring to boil. Pour hot over beans, leaving ½-inch head space. Adjust lids. Process in boiling water bath 10 minutes. Let jars stand 2 weeks for flavors to blend.

Note:
From Kathy Wages of the Clayton County (Georgia) Extension Service.

Pickled Green Tomatoes

Ingredients for 5 pints:
4 quarts green tomatoes (about 24-28
   medium-sized tomatoes)
2 cups onions, sliced
½ cup salt
2 green peppers, seeded and chopped
3 cups white *or* brown sugar
2½ Tbl. celery seed
2½ Tbl. mustard seed
2 Tbl. whole cloves
2 Tbl. whole allspice
3 3-inch sticks cinnamon
1 quart distilled white vinegar

Directions:
Wash and drain tomatoes. Peel and cut
tomatoes into slices. Peel and slice onions.
Sprinkle alternate layers of tomatoes and
onions with salt in large glass bowl. Let stand
overnight. In morning, drain well. Transfer
mixture to pan. Add peppers, sugar, celery
seed, mustard seed, and spice bag made by
placing cloves, allspice, and cinnamon in
piece of cheesecloth and tying top to secure.
Add vinegar to cover. Bring to boil. Simmer
15 minutes or until vegetables are tender.
Remove spice bag. Pack vegetables into
sterilized jars. Leave ½-inch head space. Fill
jar to within ½-inch of top with boiling hot
liquid. Remove air bubbles by sliding dull
knife around edge of jar. Adjust lids.
Process in boiling water bath 15 minutes.

Note:
   From the University of Georgia Cooper-
ative Extension Service. You can prepare
tomatoes in quarters instead of slices, if
desired.

Squash Pickles

Ingredients for 4 pints:
2 lbs. fresh zucchini squash and/or yellow
  squash
2 small onions, sliced
water
¼ cup salt
2 cups sugar
1 tsp. celery salt
1 tsp. tumeric
2 tsp. mustard seeds
3 cups cider vinegar

Directions:
Either slice squash or cut into spears. Place
squash and onions in large pot. Cover with
water. Add salt. Let mixture stand 2 hours.
Drain vegetables. Place remaining ingredients in saucepan. Bring to boil. Pour over
squash and onions in large pot. Let stand 2
hours. Bring to boil. Heat 5 minutes. Pack
squash and onions into sterilized jars. Pour
hot brine over them. Adjust lids. Process in
boiling water bath 15 minutes.

Note:
    From Pat Bruschini of the Cobb County
(Georgia) Extension Service.

Low-Sodium Pickles

Ingredients for 6 pints:
3 lbs. pickling cucumbers
3 cloves garlic
6 heads fresh dill
3 cups vinegar
3 cups water
3 tsp. salt substitute

Directions:
Wash cucumbers. Pack into sterilized jars.
Place ½ clove garlic and 1 head dill in each
jar. Heat vinegar, water, and salt substitute
in saucepan, until boiling. Cover cucumbers
with hot liquid, leaving ½ inch head space.
Adjust lids. Process 15 minutes in boiling
water bath. Allow 5 days to ripen.

Note:
    From Jean Bauerband of the Fulton
County (Georgia) Extension Service.

Bread and Butter Pickles

Ingredients for 8 pints:
25 3-5-inch long cucumbers, washed, drained, and sliced
12 medium-sized onions, sliced
2 quarts ice water
½ cup salt
1 quart vinegar
2 cups sugar
2 tsp. mustard seed
2 tsp. ground tumeric
2 tsp. celery seed

Directions:
Soak cucumbers and onions in salt solution (mix ice water with salt) 3 hours. Mix remaining ingredients. Bring to boil. Add cucumbers and onions. Heat just until boiling. Pack vegetables into jars, leaving ½-inch head space. Fill jar to within ½-inch of top with boiling hot liquid. Remove air bubbles in jars. Adjust lids. Process 5 minutes in boiling water bath.

Note:
   From Jean Bauerband of the Fulton County (Georgia) Extension Service.

Chili Powder

Ingredients:
2-3 lbs. ripe hot red peppers

Directions:
Place peppers out on kitchen counter near oven to air-dry 2 days. Then place on baking sheet in 250° oven. Dry-roast slowly, until they turn a deep, reddish brown, about 2-3 hours. Remove from oven. Cool. Crush peppers, seeds and all, with mortar and pestle. Strain through tea strainer, to remove largest seeds. Store powder in tightly covered jar.

Pear Relish

Ingredients for 4 half-pints:
2 lbs. pears, cored, peeled, and grated
1 sweet red pepper, seeded and chopped
1 large onion, chopped
1 cup sugar
½ tsp. salt
½ tsp. dry mustard
½ cup cider vinegar
¼ cup candied ginger, sliced

Directions:
In large saucepan, bring all ingredients to boil. Simmer, stirring, until thick, about 1 hour. Pour into sterilized jars and seal. Process in boiling water bath 15 minutes.

Dee's Golden Marmalade

Ingredients for 4 half-pints:
6 thick-skinned oranges, finely sliced and seeded
3 lemons, finely sliced and seeded
water, to cover
sugar (1½ times as much sugar as fruit)
1 cup lemon juice

Directions:
Place orange and lemon slices in thick-bottomed pot. Cover with water. Let stand overnight. The next morning, boil fruit and water mixture 45 minutes, stirring. Let stand overnight again. In morning, measure. Bring mixture to boil. Add 1½ times as much sugar as fruit. Bring to boil. Simmer 45 minutes, or until jelling point is reached. Just before removing from heat, add lemon juice. Pour into hot sterilized jars. Adjust lids. Process in boiling water bath 15 minutes.

Quick Cranberry Jelly

Ingredients for 6 half-pints:
3½ cups cranberry juice cocktail
1¾ ounces dry pectin
4 cups sugar
¼ cup lemon juice

Directions:
Combine cranberry juice cocktail and pectin in 6-quart saucepan. Cook over high heat, until mixture boils. Stir in sugar. Bring to full rolling boil. Boil 1 minute, stirring.

Remove from heat. Add lemon juice. Skim foam from top. Pour into sterilized jars leaving ½-inch head space. Adjust lids. Process in boiling water bath 15 minutes.

Fig Preserves

Ingredients for 10 half-pints:
7 cups sugar
¼ cup fresh lemon juice
1½ quarts hot water
2 quarts firm figs, peeled (about 4½ pounds)
2 lemons, thinly sliced

Directions:
Add sugar and lemon juice to hot water in large saucepan. Cook over low heat, until sugar dissolves. Add figs. Cook rapidly about 10 minutes, stirring. Add sliced lemons. Continue cooking rapidly about 10-15 minutes, or until figs are clear. Cover. Let stand 12-24 hours in cool place. Bring to boil again. Pour hot into sterilized jars, leaving ½-inch head space. Adjust lids. Process in boiling water bath 15 minutes.

Blueberry Jelly

Ingredients for 4 half-pints:
4 cups blueberry juice (takes about 2
    quarts blueberries and 1 cup water)
4 cups sugar

Directions:
Prepare juice: Select about ¼ slightly under-ripe and ¾ ripe berries. Sort and wash. Remove stems. Crush berries. Add water. Cover. Bring to boil in large saucepan over high heat. Reduce heat. Simmer until berries are soft. Pour cooked berries into damp jelly bag or double thickness of cheesecloth held in colander over bowl. Bring edges of cloth together. Twist tightly. Press or squeeze to extract juice. Strain juice again through damp flannel bag or 2 thicknesses of damp cheesecloth without squeezing.

Make jelly: Combine juice and sugar in large saucepan. Place over high heat. Bring to full boil, stirring. Cook mixture rapidly until thick, about 15 minutes. Remove from heat. Skim. Pour into sterilized jars, leaving ½-inch head space. Seal and process in boiling water bath 10 minutes.

Note:
From Alma, Georgia, our blueberry capital.

Peach Chutney

Ingredients for 5 pints:
4 quarts peaches, peeled, pitted and
    finely chopped
1 cup seedless raisins or 1 cup onion,
    chopped
1 hot red pepper, seeded, deveined and
    chopped
5 cups white vinegar
2-3 cups brown sugar, depending on taste
    for sweetness
¼ cup mustard seeds
2 Tbl. ground ginger
2 tsp. salt
1 clove garlic, minced

Directions:
Combine all ingredients. Cook slowly over low heat until thick, about 40 minutes. Stir frequently to prevent sticking. Pour boiling chutney into sterilized jars, leaving a ½-inch headspace. Adjust lids. Process 10 minutes in boiling water bath.

Peach Butter

Peach Preserves

Ingredients for 4 half-pints:
4 lbs. unpeeled fresh peaches, pitted and
   halved
1 cup water
dash salt
½-1 cup honey

Directions:
Slice peaches to measure 12 cups. Put in
heavy kettle with water. Bring to boil,
stirring. Simmer until tender, about 5
minutes. Press through sieve. Return peach
mixture to kettle, discarding skins. Bring to
boil. Cook briskly about 10 minutes. Reduce
heat. Simmer 20-30 minutes more, stirring
often. Add salt and honey to taste.

Cook, stirring, 10-20 minutes more, or
until amber-colored and thick on the bottom. Fill sterilized jars to within ½-inch of
top. Adjust lids. Process 15 minutes in
boiling water bath. Tighten lids.

Ingredients for 4 half-pints:
1 lb. peaches, peeled, pitted, and cut into
   halves
¾ lb. sugar
½ cup water

Directions:
Place fruit and sugar in alternate layers in
large pot. Add water. Cook over high heat,
stirring, until mixture comes to boil. Boil
rapidly, until syrup is somewhat thick. Pour
into hot, sterilized jars. Seal and process in
boiling water bath 15 minutes.

Note:
   From Sara Jones of Atlanta, an accomplished preserves and jelly maker, and
retired school teacher.

Index